Small woods on farms

A Report to the Countryside Commis~~~
by Dartington Amenity Research ~~~

Published by

Countryside Commission
John Dower House
Crescent Place
Cheltenham
Glos GL50 3RA

CCP 143

Price £7.00 net

ISBN 0 86170 035 X

K

Preface

Small woodlands are a vital part of the landscape of Britain, helping to create that unique character for which this country is famous. They are equally vital for wildlife, providing irreplaceable habitats for a wide range of species, many of which occur nowhere else but in woodland. Small woods can also be the source of valuable and renewable supplies of timber for a multitude of uses, they are important for game and sporting interests, and many are unique in their historical and archaeological importance.

Yet in recent years evidence has accumulated which suggests that many small woodlands in Britain are in a poor state through widespread neglect, poor management and misuse. Such problems were described in Westmacott and Worthington's report to the Countryside Commission in their study of landscape changes in the lowlands of England and Wales[1], and acknowledged by the Commission in their subsequent policy document[2] published in 1977. In 1976 Gwent County Council published a report[3] on the County's small woodlands which concluded that many were in a state of decline, very few were under any form of management and that, with widespread neglect and decay, their future was becoming increasingly uncertain.

The Countryside Commission followed up the initiative taken by Gwent County Council and asked Dartington Amenity Research Trust (DART) to carry out a detailed pilot survey of small woods in a small area of the Usk valley in Gwent during 1978. DART's survey confirmed the findings of Gwent County Council. It also formed the basis for an experimental project, jointly organised and financed with the Forestry Commission, to test ways of reversing the decline of small woods in eastern and central Gwent.

To discover whether the findings in Gwent were applicable to small woods generally, the survey and assessment methods tested in the pilot study were used in a wider study of small woods in England and Wales, carried out by DART in 1979. This report describes the results of their study.

All the small woods in nine carefully selected areas in England and Wales were surveyed and assessed from a number of aspects, including their contribution to landscape, nature conservation and timber production, and their sporting potential. Their future was examined in the light of their current state, their present purpose and the way they were being managed, and DART were asked to suggest ways of ensuring their future in the landscape.

The Commission believe that DART's findings should be a matter of concern to all who have an interest in the future of our countryside, and more specifically to those who have a responsibility towards the well-being of our small woodlands. We hope this report will stimulate widespread discussion of the problems and lead to measures to reverse the decline. For our part, subject to available resources, we will continue to support initiatives along the lines put forward by DART, and will press for a greater degree of commitment from all the people, organisations or bodies who are in a position to influence the future development of a valuable national resource.

Countryside Commission
February 1982

---

[1]*New Agricultural Landscapes* CCP 76 Countryside Commission 1974
[2]*New Agricultural Landscapes—Issues, Objectives and Action* CCP 102 Countryside Commission 1977
[3]*Woodland Survey Summary Report* Gwent County Council 1976

Acknowledgements

This study was carried out for the Countryside Commission by Dartington Amenity Research Trust:

Study Team

Peter Downing BA ForCert, Fiona Leney BSc PhD, Andrew Cowen DipAD HND.
Drafting: Sheila Sherris. Secretary: Diana Hunt.

Field Surveyors

Malcolm Cowper HND, Charles Driver BSc MSc, Justin Gilbert BSc, Geoffrey Morgan BSc MSc DipEd, Margaret Nixon BSc, Howard Rice BA MSc, Rebecca Roberts, Julia Webber, Raymond Youell HND MSc

Consultants

Lucy Huntington BSc DipLDesign, Lionel Kelleway BSc

In addition to the farmers and landowners who were so generous with their time and who granted access to their woodlands, grateful thanks are due to the following organisations, firms and individuals for background information and their comments on the draft report:

Government Bodies

Countryside Commission (Headquarters and Regional Staff), Department of the Environment (Directorate of Rural Affairs), Forestry Commission (Headquarters, Conservancy, Research and Estates Staff), Institute of Terrestrial Ecology, Ministry of Agriculture (Agricultural Development and Advisory Service), Nature Conservancy Council

County Planning Departments

Cambridgeshire, Clwyd, Cornwall, East Sussex, Essex, Gwent, Hampshire, Hereford and Worcester, Leicestershire, Lincolnshire, Norfolk, North Yorkshire, Oxfordshire, Shropshire, Somerset, Staffordshire, Suffolk, Warwickshire, Wiltshire

National Organisations

Centre for Agricultural Strategy, Country Landowners' Association, Farmers' Union of Wales, Farming and Wildlife Advisory Group, Home Grown Timber Merchants' Association, National Farmers' Union, Royal Institution of Chartered Surveyors, Royal Society for the Protection of Birds, Royal Society for Nature Conservation, Tree Council, Woodland Trust, Timber Research and Development Association

Land Agents and Consultants

Chris Yarrow and Associates, Clifford Dann and Partners, Cluttons, Rural Planning Services Ltd, Stratton and Holborrow, Turner and Fletcher

Timber Processors, Agents, etc

Ashton Paper Mill Ltd, Baltic Sawmills Ltd, Blackman, Pavie and Ladden Ltd, Bowater-Scott Ltd, Ben Evans and Co, Caerwys Sawmills, Coalition Coal and Shipping Co, Cubbington Sawmill, Dartington Sawmills Ltd, T R Deeble, Duchy of Cornwall Woodlands, R E Duffield, R B Eley, Glynn Valley Timber Co, James Joiner and Sons Ltd, John Boddy and Son (Timber) Ltd, John Stenning and Son Ltd, Norsdale Sawmill, Prestwood and Son (Horncastle) Ltd, Revelstoke Woodlands, D Stephens, Tavistock Woodlands Ltd, J Thoms, Western Woodland Owners Ltd, W G Gould and Sons Ltd, W J Hooper and Sons

Individuals

Dr H C Dawkins, Commonwealth Forestry Institute, University of Oxford, Professor J Matthews, Department of Forestry, University of Aberdeen, Dr H Newby, Department of Sociology, University of Essex, Dr R Lorraine-Smith, Department of Environmental Resources, University of Bradford, Mr C Watkins, Department of Geography, University of Nottingham

The maps in this report are based on the Ordnance Survey Maps, with the sanction of the Controller of HM Stationery Office. Crown copyright reserved.

Contents

Appendices

Figures

Maps of The Study Areas

1 Introduction

1.1   The origins of this study lie in the action taken by the Countryside Commission as a result of repeated expressions of strong public concern at the changes which have taken place in the landscape of lowland Britain over the last thirty years. This concern and the debate about causes and remedies is well known and amply documented (for example, references [41], [43] and [45]*).

1.2   In their report *New Agricultural Landscapes* [74], Westmacott and Worthington confirmed that much of the familiar landscape was likely to change in the medium and long term. They recommended some positive conservation measures where such action was still possible, and suggested ways of making new landscapes more attractive. A key point was that trees and small woods are, with hedgerows, the most important visual elements of the landscapes studied. The Commission's own policy document, *New Agricultural Landscapes: Issues, Objectives, and Action* [7] specified the need to promote new research into landscape conservation problems.

1.3   At first the Commission concentrated their attention on the general consequences of landscape decline arising out of the Westmacott and Worthington study and gave priority to grant aiding tree planting schemes. Then, in 1975, they asked DART to examine a sample of the planting schemes which had been carried out. DART reported to the Commission in 1976 [9]. Our research also suggested the need for policies, advice and, perhaps, grant-aid for *existing* small woodlands. The Forestry Commission has estimated [22] that a significant proportion of the 329,000 hectares of high forest in England and Wales is made up of small woodlands on farms, and, in addition, there are 231,000 hectares of coppice-with-standards, coppice and scrub woodland. Clearly, the conservation of existing but at present unmanaged woodland was a matter worthy of research.

1.4   DART were then asked to make proposals for a new research project to investigate the current condition of small woodlands on farms. After discussion the proposals were hardened into a new study, the scope and content of which is given in detail below and in Appendices I and II. The progress of the study was monitored by a steering group made up of representatives from a wide range of landowning, farming, conservation and statutory interests.

1.5   To understand properly the importance of small woods it is necessary to be aware of their function in the countryside. This can be roughly divided into five main headings:

i.   Landscape

Small woodlands are a vital component of the landscape of much of lowland England and Wales, and, indeed, of many upland areas. They add immeasurably to the diversity of the scene by complementing the pattern of hedgerows and the topography of river valleys and stream sides, and by balancing larger woodlands. They occur, with variations in size, shape and character, in all landscape types from the flat horizons of the east, through the rolling chalk and limestone areas of central England to the sheltered combes and hidden valleys of the west and Wales. Their importance to the scene can never be underestimated whether in national parks, intensively cultivated land or even in the urban fringe. With the demise of a huge number of trees through diseases such as Dutch elm and beech bark and the consequences of modern agricultural practices (including the loss of a great many hedgerow trees), the place of small woodlands as prominent features in the landscape is now more important than ever before. A number of small woods have been lost to the landscape in many areas, and, if this loss, for whatever reasons, becomes greater, then there will be serious consequences for the future character of our landscape, most notably an unacceptable spread of visually dull and uninteresting tracts of countryside.

ii.   Wildlife Conservation

The concern for the declining landscapes is closely bound up with anxiety about the implications for wildlife conservation, especially the disturbing effects of environmental pollution (most notably expressed by Carson [5]) and the rapid disappearance of habitats such as existing woodland (particu-

---

*For references see Appendix IV, page 103

larly the relics of the ancient forests) noted by biological scientists and other informed observers (see for example [59] and [63], and [10], [50] and [73]). This added an important dimension to the study which could not be overlooked.

iii. Timber Production

Foresters, timber merchants, many landowners, and some journalists frequently comment on the potential of small woodlands as part of our national timber resources. This must be viewed both against the broad context of global timber resources and the more narrow one of local decision making in land management. Both the Forestry Commission and the Centre for Agricultural Strategy have made a case, based on examinations of the need for timber in the twenty-first century, for a substantial increase in forestry ([27] and [6]), and although their attention is directed mainly towards the uplands there is no doubt that lowland woods would also be affected by any major change in forest policy. Even without this new pressure for a change in policy, the post-World War II decades have seen considerable changes in woodland management [46]: of the 'high forest' in Britain in 1965, some 55 per cent was classified as 'broadleaved' [38]; in 1971, the rate of planting and replanting by private owners was about 23,000 hectares a year, mostly replanting existing woods [19]; and Simpson refers to the trend of replacing broadleaved crops with conifers [66]. Although contemporary figures are awaited from the results of the Forestry Commission's national tree survey, due in the early 1980s, it is probable that the ratio of broadleaf to conifer species has declined substantially, and that the overall planting rate has also declined.

iv. Historical and Archaeological Heritage

In addition to the conservation issue there is the related one of historical and archaeological value. The case for viewing woods, parks, and hedgerow trees as artefacts from our cultural, agricultural and industrial past has been strongly made ([63], [50] and [36]), the argument being that certain woods typifying different historical conditions and economic systems should be regarded in the same light, and be subject to the same conservation criteria, as historic buildings.

v. Game Conservation

Finally, the Countryside Commission were aware of the importance in many areas of small woodlands for field sports—the inital work in their Demonstration Farms Project, has shown this clearly, as has the experience of the Game Conservancy ([30], for example)—which further adds to the complexities attached to the multiple use of woodland.

1.6   Against this background, DART were asked to investigate the problems of small woodlands on farmland, and in the light of their findings to suggest ways in which they could be managed and conserved *without*:

    i.   making excessive calls on farmers' resources;

    ii.   removing the basic responsibility for care of these features out of farmers' and owners' hands;

    iii.   adding to, or distorting, the present administrative arrangements for countryside planning and management;

    iv.   necessitating massive grant-aid.

1.7   The terms of reference of the study were:

    i.   to establish the extent and nature of existing small woodlands on farms;

    ii.   to establish the extent of farmers' knowledge and understanding of their existing woodlands;

    iii.   to establish the attitudes of farmers to their woodlands;

    iv.   to estimate the value of woodlands under a range of headings: landscape, wildlife conservation, historical, timber production, game;

    v.   on stated assumptions concerning objectives, to determine what work is required to manage woodlands effectively, and the mechanisms whereby this might be carried out;

    vi.   to state in broad terms what calls this would make on farmers' time, money and entrepreneurial ability, and how they might best be assisted;

vii.   to state what other factors, outside the farmers' control, appear to cause difficulties, and to suggest how they might be overcome;

viii.   to assess the extent to which the economics of managing small woods might be influenced by technical developments in forestry.

1.8   Discussions were held with the Commission and with:

i.   officers of the Forestry Commission's Research and Development Division;

ii.   officers of the Nature Conservancy Council and the Institute of Terrestrial Ecology;

iii.   representatives of farmers' and landowners' organisations;

iv.   officers of the Timber Growers' Organisation and the Home Grown Timber Merchants' Association;

v.   officers from the planning departments of three county councils known to have a special interest in small woods and their management: East Sussex, Essex and Gwent.

1.9   It was decided that, following the experience of the *New Agricultural Landscapes* study [74], a series of case studies centred on well-wooded areas in eight counties should be carried out, preceded by a pilot project in Gwent to test out the study methods (Appendix I). A statistically valid sample was not sought, but the aim was to include some representation of the range of:

i.   agricultural conditions and practices in England and Wales;

ii.   farming structures (the sizes, ownerships, and occupancies of holdings);

iii.   socio-economic factors associated with farming;

iv.   sizes, types and functions of woodlands in England and Wales.

1.10   The nine counties chosen (including the pilot county, Gwent) are listed below. Selection was made in the light of financial resources available at the time.

Cambridgeshire	East Sussex	North Yorkshire
Clwyd	Gwent (pilot study area)	Somerset
Cornwall	Lincolnshire	Warwickshire

1.11   Two small study areas were chosen in each county in consultation with the County Planning Department: a first choice and a reserve area. The latter was included in case of serious problems arising in the area first chosen (a change of area was necessary only in Clwyd, where the first choice proved to be largely under one ownership). The criteria for the final choice of area was that it should:

i.   be a lowland area;

ii.   constitute a broadly homogenous landscape unit (ie bounded by roads or natural features);

iii.   include at least eight woodlands under separate ownership;

iv.   have a number and area of woods capable of being surveyed within the financial and manpower resources available;

v.   include a reasonable representation of the county's woodland types.

(In an area of predominantly large holdings but small woodlands, the net had to be cast uncomfortably wide to achieve objectives iii, iv and v. This is borne out by the case study maps and data, and, indeed, final decisions on boundaries had to be deferred until quite a late point in the survey period.)

1.12   The study areas are shown on Figure 1. They encompass a wide range of farming and woodland conditions. The research, its findings, conclusions and recommendations were presented in a draft report to the Countryside Commission in January 1980, and were widely circulated to government departments and agencies, local government planning departments, organisations with forestry, timber and amenity interests, and a number of people in academic institutions. Their comments and criticisms have been taken into account in preparing this report.

1.13   Mention should be made of the pilot study in Gwent and its outcome. The research was reported to the Countryside Commission in June 1978. As a result of its recommendations, a project officer was appointed to work in the area close to that studied, working with farmers, farmers' organisations, local authorities and other statutory bodies, and conservation and amenity organisations, to improve the way small woodlands were being used, taking into account the constraints of wildlife and landscape conservation. The project was initially funded and managed by the Forestry Commission, but is now funded jointly by the Forestry and Countryside Commissions. It will be the subject of a future report.

1.14   The survey was therefore extensive and broad-based. As is the nature of such surveys, the unkind critic might describe it as a 'once over, lightly'. The field survey teams, although trained and from appropriate disciplines, were non-specialist. The individual appraisals, if conducted by specialists for one purpose only, would probably have been more detailed and rigorous, for example, a timber buyer might well have measured every standard of wood. There were missing dimensions to the research, as with the lack of ornithological surveys (although the autumn and winter timing of the fieldwork would have made this difficult in any case) and the lack of detailed research into the botanical history of each wood; and the timber values have been based on assumptions which are debatable, although they have been amended in the light of criticism of the results of the first stage. However, its merits outweigh these deficiencies by a considerable margin. Over 500 pieces of woodland were examined in widely varying bio- and socio-geographic conditions and areas. The woods were appraised simultaneously and at a fixed point in their evolution or other process of change.

1.15   This study is possibly unique—it is certainly valuable. We hope its findings and conclusions will contribute to understanding and securing a more assured future for one of the most important features of our countryside—the small woods.

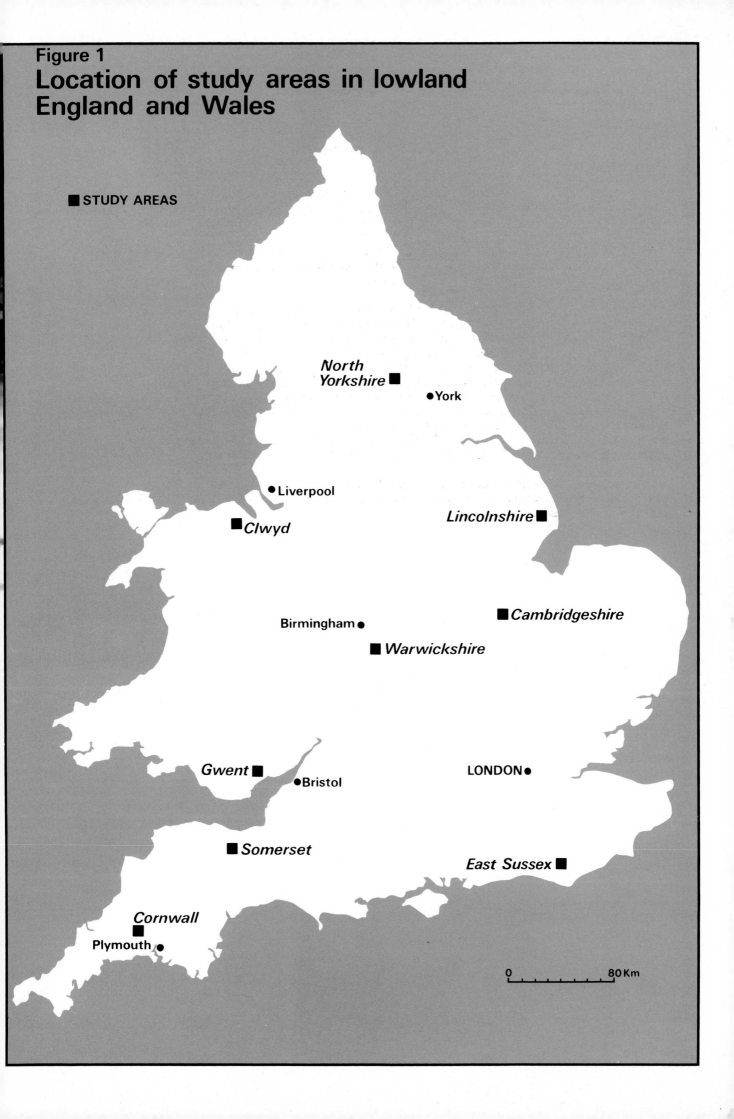

Figure 1
Location of study areas in lowland England and Wales

■ STUDY AREAS

North Yorkshire ■

●York

●Liverpool

■ Clwyd

Lincolnshire ■

■ Cambridgeshire

Birmingham ●

■ Warwickshire

Gwent ■

●Bristol

LONDON ●

■ Somerset

East Sussex ■

Cornwall ■

Plymouth ●

0   80 Km

2   The Conclusions

2.1   **Our main conclusion is that the small woods of England and Wales found mainly on farmland are a considerable and (to an extent) quantifiable asset which is badly used and whose value for a range of purposes is diminishing as a result. We feel that steps must be taken to reverse this deterioration, and that a more positive programme than currently exists is needed. Although it would necessarily involve a long-term commitment, both the environment and the economy would benefit. However, no solution at all will be possible unless all those with an interest in small woods can be persuaded that they are an important but deteriorating material resource, that steps should be taken to reverse their decline, and that all concerned should work together to put matters right. The findings below are related first to the study's terms of reference; conclusions are then drawn in a wider context.**

Nature and Extent

2.2   In our view the small woodlands in the study areas are representative of those in England and Wales as a whole. Almost all cover less than ten hectares, and two-thirds cover less than one hectare. They are on land which is mostly unsuited to agriculture. They are made up predominantly of broadleaved trees but with a frequent admixture of conifers from past management efforts, although the 10 per cent which had been fairly recently replanted were mostly coniferous. Their extent cannot be accurately stated until the Forestry Commission's woodland census is completed; the best estimate at present is about 340,000 hectares.

Farmers' Knowledge and Attitudes

2.3   Only about 1 per cent of the farmers and landowners interviewed had enough basic knowledge to manage their woodlands effectively. Since up to 10 per cent of the study areas are under woodland cover this is unfortunate, but not surprising. Apart from among a few landowners and their agents, woodland management is not a traditional activity for either owner-occupier or tenant farmers. However, there is no lack of interest if the requisite information can be made available. This unsatisfactory level of knowledge is linked to a strong ambivalence towards woods. There is a considerable element of sympathy towards woods as part of the local environment, but this is coupled with a lack of realisation of their values and their management needs—most farmers are not fully aware of their woods or that they demand attention.

2.4   Only when the need for effective management is explained, or attention is drawn to woods (such as by way of our interviews), do the prevailing attitudes begin to sharpen. These attitudes can readily be changed, positively for the most part, through interest and advice.

The Values of Small Woodlands

2.5   **Landscape.** In all but two study areas, woodlands are an integral part of the landscape, accentuating its topographic features, softening the angularities of roads, buildings and fields and providing essential diversity and contrast in the scene. Where less directly related to the landscape, they are still of strong visual importance, and their absence would be considered detrimental by most of those who live in or visit the areas. Directly or indirectly, they give immense visual pleasure.

2.6   **Wildlife.** We cannot state exactly what proportion of the woods surveyed are really ancient, but there are such woods in every area studied and we believe the total proportion to be quite significant. We stress in Chapters 4 and 5 the incalculable value of these relict woodlands and the need for conservation to be the prime objective. The many other woods which are not ancient still have considerable value as habitats for a wide range of wildlife, and also in some instances as protectors of other non-woodland habitats, for example grassland.

2.7   **Historical.** Our terms of reference did not include a full appraisal of the historical value of the woods in the study areas, but it is evident that a proportion of them are of sufficient value,—in terms of their origins as artefacts or as hiding ancient earthworks—to merit long-term conservation. Their recorded numbers and values are not as high as for wildlife, but they are locally significant, and since their age is often the reason for them sustaining a wildlife value this aspect of woodland conservation deserves more attention.

2.8   **Timber.** In Chapter 5 we show that, despite their dilapidated state, most woods do have a monetary value: this is confirmed by the eagerness with which our research was greeted by a number of timber merchants. That value accrues to the farmer or landowner. The estimated value of the 629 hectares of unmanaged woodland (which includes a high proportion of coppice and scrub) which we surveyed averages £1,332 per hectare. If this figure for the study areas is regarded as a reliable average applicable to the whole of England and Wales then such woodlands may be worth—to the farmers or landowners on standing values—around £450 million. These woods are therefore a significant and under-used national resource. Although it is a tiny sum in comparison with the annual turnover in the agricultural industry, it is locally very valuable and, carefully tapped, could could realise useful capital. More important, perhaps, if they had been maintained properly then their value would be many times higher.

2.9   **Game.** Because of the secrecy with which this subject tends to be shrouded we have been unable to assess the monetary value of small woods for game conservation. However, we can say that shooting is a multi-million pound industry and woodlands are vital to its continuance. Also, the potential value of game conservation on farmland, whether for personal enjoyment or for commercial gain, is only partly realised and there is much scope for increasing the quantity and quality of sporting opportunities.

Future Management

2.10   The four main aspects of conservation in Britain have been listed by Cobham and Leonard [41] as historical, wildlife, aesthetic and recreational: their objectives being "too diverse and conflicting for simple reconciliation measures to be successful". This opinion is expressed by the writers in respect of conflict between farming and conservation. The same four aspects also relate to small woods on farmland but, as is shown in later chapters, it should be possible to reconcile the differing objectives of conservation interests and of farmers to a considerable degree. On the farmers' side, there is much less interest apparent in the pursuit of profit on their woods than on their agricultural enterprises. The majority of farmers interviewed valued their woods for exactly the same reasons as the non-farming public, and showed some interest in managing them to those ends.

2.11   From the point of view of those pressing for more effective conservation, the evidence we have accumulated points to an unsatisfactory condition of most woods surveyed. There are problems of dereliction and deterioration which will significantly reduce the landscape, wildlife, historical and recreational values of woods to society, with even clearance or disappearance occurring here and there. As stated in Chapter 1, the sample of woods surveyed is not statistically valid, but nothing read, seen, or heard about woods elsewhere leads us to believe that the areas studied are not reasonably representative of the nation's small woods generally.

2.12   One of the most difficult things to do, in an unsatisfactory situation such as this, is to define the problem: our view is that the areas of concern discussed in this report are symptoms rather than the cause of the current decline. We believe that the real problem is this: we no longer make proper use of our lowland, predominantly broadleaved, woods. This report suggests some reasons: the dwindling or collapse of traditional markets for woodland produce; the historic shift in land tenure; the severing of links between farmers and potential markets; the failure of rural enterprise to adjust to changed market situations; and the altered perceptions of forestry objectives in the post-war period. These, combined with a rise in agricultural prosperity in the post-war period, have led to a view by farmers and foresters alike that small woods are relatively useless, non-functional relics of a bygone age. In fact, the symptoms constitute a syndrome, and looked at in this way the problem should be capable of being solved. It follows that bringing back small woodlands under what is very loosely called 'management' would go a long way towards reversing the present decline, and in fact the marketing of woodland produce is perhaps a key element in any programme for improving their condition. Chapters 4 and 5, show that it is perfectly possible to manage woods for ends which differ wood by wood, but which:

  i.   collectively satisfy the different interest groups noted in paragraph 2.10;

  ii. show that woods on farms can pay their way and so still have a function in the late twentieth century.

2.13   Where small woods have a high conservation value, we believe that any new management policies should defer to conservation. But within that constraint, they should be managed for the production of utilisable wood for commercial markets, bearing in mind that such markets are capable of being extended to include new products. In Chapter 4 we give examples of different management approaches to accommodate varying regional characteristics (paragraphs 4.51 to 4.55), and in Chapter 5 we demonstrate the wide range of options open to the woodland manager (paragraphs 5.33 to 5.38). There are two critical elements: the style of management must suit the objectives of the farmer or landowner, and it must be tailored to the site. We suggest later some mechanisms whereby this might be brought about.

Calls on Farmers' Resources

2.14   Depending on their timber value and on any local conservation constraints, bringing woods into production need make no direct call on the farm budget—indeed the operation can pay for itself (paragraph 5.35). However, the farmer may have to forego some income and must be prepared to spend at least a little time on managing his woods. Within the range of possible management approaches between the two extremes of complete replanting (paragraph 5.38) and an *ad hoc* selection system (paragraph 5.36), the farmer balances the demands for money with those of time. Therefore, if he retains full control of his woods, then there will be substantial calls on one or other (unless he can come to an arrangement with an outside person or body—see next chapter) in establishing a management regime.

2.15   Farmers or landowners managing their own woods would also need some entrepreneurial skill, but of no different kind or degree to that needed for farming. However, the vast majority of farmers do not have the necessary background in the forest produce market to perform this entrepreneurial role well, and might find it expensive to acquire. It is here that help would be most needed and welcomed, and we suggest a way of supplying it in the next chapter.

Other Problems

2.16   Apart from the problems already mentioned, notably quality of advice, reliable access to timber markets, and finance, we believe that there are no special factors outside the farmer's control which appear to cause difficulties: the weather, whilst important, is usually more troublesome to agricultural rather than woodland enterprises. However, there is one aspect of finance which is very important. As a nation, we have decided that there are advantages in having trees and woods. This is recognised by the tax laws mentioned in paragraph 5.40, by the grants noted in paragraphs 4.2 and 4.3, by the Nature Conservancy Council in providing funds to safeguard, in selected cases, the scientific value of woods, and by some counties where there is some finance available from the local authority to protect their historical value. However, this funding is somewhat piecemeal and inadequate and there are Treasury rules against 'topping up' one grant with another. Bearing in mind the wide differences in circumstances, which are exemplified in Chapter 5, some new, better integrated, and more flexible form of assistance is urgently required.

Technical Developments

2.17   Our desk research shows that technical developments in forestry appear to be largely irrelevant to the economics of small woodlands (paragraphs 2.23 to 2.25). Although there is some current interest in the free growth of oak [37] (which is an encouragement to those who aim for higher profits by keeping an open canopy) the technical developments most likely to affect the economics of small woods are concerned with utilisation. Most notable are trends in which formerly valueless produce acquires a new market in some areas. Examples are:

    i.   improvements to hardwood pulp processes so that a wider range of species, billet sizes, and a higher bark percentage are acceptable. (Thus large hazel coppice wood and scrub birch are now taken at one mill);

    ii.   the development of a wood chip industry with ultimate uses in the livestock industry and as packing (this market can take a wide range of species and almost any size of smallwood—and there are prototype chippers for farm tractors which make it possible for the farmer to process and use his own timber);

    iii.   the considerable increase in popularity of wood-burning stoves which are economical to run and are rapidly expanding the market for firewood;

    iv.   the potential (now being researched) for 'wood energy' plantations (for farm gate sales to processors who would use the wood to extract methanol).

The Wider Context

2.18   One of the aims of this study is to comment on the woodland policies currently followed by the Country-side Commission and other agencies. As these are national policies, some discussion of conservation in the wider national context is necessary. The continuing public debate on the conflict between intensive agriculture and environmental conservation, although important in itself, is really part of an increased interest in and wider debate about the future of the countryside, including settlements, industry, and rural society, which has been stimulated by the Countryside Review Committee's Discussion Paper [8]. It follows that the future of small woodlands—most of which are on farms—must be seen in terms of their social and economic policy context as well as in terms of conservation. And this must in turn be set within the increasing international awareness of finite world resources and the increasing costs of energy and raw materials. It is outside our terms of reference to attempt any synthesis of these debates, conflicts, and complex forces, but we wish to draw attention to the relevance of the findings of this study to the rural economy and to the conservation of natural resources.

2.19   **Rural Economy.** In paragraph 2.8 it is estimated that, standing, the small woods in England and Wales are worth around £450 million. However, they are also valuable in terms of the employment they could generate for timber contractors and saw-mill workers. There are several hundred saw mills which are almost entirely dependent on home-grown timber, but for the most part they are located some distance from the important areas of afforestation [11]. We have noted that the supply of home-grown timber reaching the market is erratic, and with the dwindling of elm supplies the future for the industry is poor. Although we have no figures on the numbers employed, on the current trend it seems that future losses of jobs are likely. However, this need not be inevitable. It is our understanding from talks with saw-mills, pulp companies and the Council for Small Industries in Rural Areas (CoSIRA) that the industry would welcome and co-operate with action to bring small woods under better management. CoSIRA estimates that £10,000 worth of sales are needed to justify each 'marginal' job in the timber industry. Converting this back (conservatively) to trees, it probably represents about 500 cubic metres (or for 'up market' products as little as 200 cubic metres) of standing timber per job. Thus in each study area the volumes of wood and other products summarised in Table 3 (page 32) would create or save the amount of employment given in Table 1.

Table 1   Rough Estimates of Marginal Employment Implied by Figures for Standing Volumes in Table 3

Study Area	Man-years[1]	Study Area	Man-years[1]
Cambridgeshire	23.2	Lincolnshire	21.5
Clwyd	8.8	North Yorkshire	9.3
Cornwall	17.4	Somerset	15.6
East Sussex	24.9	Warwickshire	14.2
Gwent	11.5		

[1]Rounded down to nearest tenth of a year

2.20   Some of the standing volumes on which these figures are based are in the smaller woods which are estimated to have no value for sale. On the other hand, other woods include high quality timber which probably offsets this in this crude calculation. Taking it further to produce a notional figure for the country as a whole cannot be done directly (since clearfelling every wood in the country cannot be contemplated), but a very rough estimate can be obtained another way. Taking an average annual yield of timber as 8 cubic metres per hectare (see Table 2, page 32) and the 500 cubic metres of standing timber per job estimate from the previous paragraph, then perhaps another 640 people could be employed on a sustained yield basis if the unmanaged woods were brought into use. In addition to these saw-mill workers, employment would also be generated for several hundred contractors.

2.21   Nor does this complete the employment picture. The woodland grants noted elsewhere also generate (or help retain) employment in the forestry contracting industry and the horticultural industry. We have no means of quantifying this, and the whole question of employment multipliers in forest-based industries seems to us to be in urgent need of research. However, successive governments have continued with a rural develop-ment policy which seeks to combat rural depopulation [34], and the Development Commission have been charged with the task of generating about 1,500 new employment opportunities per year [15]. Although the jobs noted above would scarcely meet this objective, in terms of their location they would be important as they are essentially rural in nature. Therefore the grants and other help for woodland owners can be matched by financial assistance to the timber industry.

2.22   The case for forestry as a generator of rural employment and as an alternative land use to agriculture is put forward in papers [12], [13] and [33]. These, particularly the last, indicate that forestry is an expensive means of generating primary rural employment; hence the accent, from 1975 onwards, on industrial employment in rural areas. However, the calculations are based on extensive afforestation in the uplands, and the same parameters do not apply to small woods in the lowlands, which are already under trees and from which there are acknowledged and financially recognised benefits from landscape and wildlife conservation. It is true to say therefore that the employment opportunities which could occur from the better management of small woods form only a part of the overall benefit accruing from making better use of this resource.

2.23   **Forest Economics.** The standard economic arguments for and against forestry are worth a small digression. The standard criteria for judging the worth of a forest investment are, as with other investment decisions, the internal rate of return (IRR) and the net discounted revenue (NDR). (Interestingly, it was a forester who pioneered the use of these techniques [40]). These calculate the flow of costs and benefits over the life of a stand of trees, and use compound interest to express them as a net percentage on investment (IRR), or as the present value of the net profit (NDR). Looked at this way, forestry is not very profitable (hence the offsetting tax concessions and grants). For example one oak wood in the survey, now valued at around £52,000, if discounted over an optimistic 150 years at 5 per cent compound interest, would have had a 'present value' to its owner all those years ago of only £34.48. If the owner had spent more than this sum (at its 1979 value), it would actually have meant a loss on the original investment.

2.24   We intend no criticism of this valuable management decision tool, but we suggest that as far as the small woods in this survey are concerned it is irrelevant. First, they are there already, so the original investment decision does not apply. Second the apparent simplicity of discounting techniques disguises the psychological complexity of the decisions. Farmers used to thinking of a yield from an agricultural enterprise within four to five years' time, do not easily comprehend even a short timber rotation of, say, twenty-five years; they tend to work more on a cash flow basis. Of course, they do their sums with care, and so it is not a point of ignorance but one of perception. For example, it is certain that few farmers with woods of timber value would bother searching through the farm records to see what it cost to establish them.

2.25   Third, there is the size of the woods. Few of those surveyed came into the Forestry Commission's potentially profitable Basis III category, and, other things being equal, they are too small to be profitable in NDR or IRR terms, regardless of how they are managed. Yet it is desirable (and most farmers would agree) that they should be brought under management of some sort. Finally there is the fact, explored in Chapter 6, that most farmers are not interested in profit from their woods in the classic economic sense. They are, however, interested in the possibility of some cash flow—an expression used periodically during this report is that the woods should "pay their way". We conclude that the financial parameters for managing small woods are not necessarily the maximisation of revenue (as in large-scale afforestation), but could instead be:

> to optimise cash flow within landscape and wildlife constraints;

> to maximise wildlife or landscape values within given cash-flow constraints;

> to minimise cash and labour inputs to maintain an existing woodland condition;

all of which are perfectly rational and echo strongly the feelings expressed by many farmers. Thus farmers and landowners may invest money in small woodlands without necessarily looking for a commercial rate of return.

2.26   **Conservation of Resources.** Yet another part of the overall benefit from re-establishing sound management practice is the self-renewing nature of native woods. Unless they are grubbed up or badly abused they keep on growing and, if properly cropped, can produce a sustained yield indefinitely. The wise use of the earth's resources has long been a matter of debate and has been a matter of government policy and action, at least since the United Nations Conference on the Human Environment in 1972 [14]. Depletion of the world's forests is one source of concern and, although the Forestry Commission [27] takes a cautiously optimistic view, that is not shared by, for example, the Centre for Agricultural Strategy [6].

2.27   Small woods cannot hope to account for more than a tiny fraction of the national demand for timber (although there is room for further substitution [69]); but, in the arguments about further large-scale afforestation, it should not be forgotten that they exist; that they are already a significant source of quality hardwoods; and that they could, by being effectively managed, produce much more than they do now. The estimated 46,000 tonnes of firewood (Table 3) the study areas could supply (if clearfelled) would be a by-product and would not solve the nation's energy problems. But such woods could be important local sources of fuel, bearing in mind the extra costs of haulage to remote rural areas, and represent the equivalent of 17,000 tonnes of coal. Again, they are a renewable resource and, over the country as a whole, could be developed as a significant source of energy.

3 Recommendations

3.1   **The aim of the study was to examine ways in which existing small woods on farmland could be managed and conserved, without:**

    i.   **making excessive calls on farmers' resources;**

    ii.   **removing the basic responsibility for their care out of farmers' and landowners' hands;**

    iii.   **adding to, or distorting, the present administrative arrangements for countryside management;**

    v.   **necessitating massive grant-aid.**

Because of the many different aspects of small woods which need to be taken into account, and because of the many different vested interests in each of those aspects, it is not possible to put forward a simple programme for reversing their decline and improving their condition—each wood needs to be assessed individually. An added complication is the uncertainty currently surrounding the future direction and policies of a number of the statutory bodies who have responsibilities covering small woods. These bodies would play a key role in promoting rehabilitation work. The recommendations in this chapter are made bearing in mind these difficulties and the above constraints.

The Options

3.2   Since markets for woodland produce do exist, and since we recommend the restoration of the productive capability of small woods, it is tempting to think that simply bringing together markets and woodland owners would be enough to start the process of recovery. Unfortunately, although a necessary condition, this connection would not in itself be sufficient for a number of reasons. First, we are reasonably certain that the initiative must be taken to farmers and landowners: where woodlands are concerned they are much more likely to be passive than active. Second, the real value of woods lies in their aggregation within an area or district, whereas those farmers and landowners who would be prepared to take the lead are few and far between. It would be sensible therefore to try to secure some economy of scale by working systematically over an area with farmers having the option to participate or not. This again suggests a need to go to all the farmers in a chosen area.

3.3   Third, we show later that most woods need to be managed at a level beyond the capability of the timber trade: it does not have the skills and, it could be argued, would be put in the position of running with the hare and hunting with the hounds. Also, some woods, perhaps most, are too valuable for wildlife, landscape, and game conservation to be left to the risk of inexpert management. The fourth problem lies in the adverse experiences reported by a number of farmers: they do not trust timber contractors, and a lot of painstaking work is needed to restore their confidence. Fifth, it is essential to approach woodland management with a high degree of sensitivity to particular wildlife and historical values, and it is inevitable that the more valuable woods will need specialist advice and expertise to deal with these aspects. Finally, as we have already noted, the timber trade are not interested in many woods because of their low values and potential yield in the present circumstances. In some areas not only are the total values low but, as in Cornwall, saw-mills do not have the capacity (or the local sawn-timber markets) to cope with increased supplies of timber and other produce, and alternative approaches must be found.

3.4   There are no easy answers. Harvesting timber may prove attractive, but many farmers will be reluctant to do more than this if there are longer-term expenses and overhead costs; and there is a massive apathy to overcome. Nevertheless, there is a small but significant minority of farmers and landowners, some well known and respected locally, who are willing to take on more woodland management. Where they go, others will eventually follow. In the paragraphs below we attempt to show how different approaches, at different levels, can be used. It should be borne in mind that the problems of small woods are determined by social as well as economic factors, and that action is needed on both fronts if any impact is to be made.

Project Officers

3.5   We believe that the best solution to the problem is to employ project officers to work in (and outwards from) specific areas, beginning perhaps, in the areas surveyed in this study, where interest has already been aroused. We believe that their work, that of stimulating interest and winning trust, should be confined to a specified area, at least during the early stages, and time and effort should not be wasted by following up casual enquiries from a whole region. We strongly recommend that they should be qualified foresters, because, although interest in woodlands can readily be aroused by others with different backgrounds, professional and technical forestry advice is almost always needed, and is at the heart of the solution to most woodland problems.

3.6   However, a training in forestry will not in itself be enough since, although technical expertise in forestry management and marketing is essential, many foresters are set in their ways and find difficulty in managing woods for anything other than commercial purposes, often relying on a narrow range of techniques. The project officers would need to be capable of using a wide variety of forestry and woodland management skills and be adept at stimulating others into action. They would also need to be widely experienced and knowledgeable about a range of countryside issues. Flexibility of objective, advice and interpretation would be the principal aim of the work. The following is a suggested brief for such a project officer. He or she would be expected to:

    i.   make contact with farmers and landowners in the selected area, preferably through local farming organisations and other established channels, in order to:

        a.   establish an initial rapport;

        b.   make an early examination of the woodlands to appraise their condition and rough timber value and the need for specialised advice on their landscape and wildlife value;

        c.   obtain, on the basis of that appraisal, the views of farmers and landowners, and discuss possible approaches to secure better management of their woods;

        d.   seek specialised advice, if necessary;

    ii.   liaise with a variety of bodies which have responsibilities for woodlands or conservation, and from which advice can be sought, for example:

        a.   Forestry Commission, Agricultural Development and Advisory Service, Nature Conservancy Council, Countryside Commission;

        b.   local authorities;

        c.   Farming and Wildlife Advisory Group;

        d.   County Trust for Nature Conservation;

        e.   academic institutions with expertise in aspects of woodlands;

    iii. prepare and agree a simple plan of operations with farmers or landowners

        a.   tailored to their objectives, resources, and the woodlands concerned;

        b.   matching, where possible, plans of operations agreed with other farmers in the vicinity, with the eventual aim of establishing some form of woodland plan for the whole area, which would bring economic benefits due to the scale of operation and co-operation in the use of resources;

    iv. provide impartial but informed advice to farmers on:

        a.   harvesting and marketing;

        b.   any forestry works and services needed to rehabilitate woodlands.

3.7   The work would call for considerable professional and technical skills and experience in forestry and the timber market, and experience in conservation management, for example, recognition of and action to safeguard wildlife habitats, landscape, historical and archaeological features. Such qualifications are not common, but suitable people are available or could be trained in the missing skills. The project officers would also need considerable social skills and the ability to place themselves in and understand the other person's position.

3.8   The project officers' work would need to continue for a period of years because real headway will take time. On past evidence, many farmers will be cautious—and rightly so. So too will the timber trade and the two sorts of contractors (for harvesting and new forest works), especially where new investment is concerned. However, we believe this wariness will last for the medium-term only in any one area. Once set up, market forces should be a strong enough incentive for the system to run smoothly—and, like other innovations, the effects should ripple outwards.

3.9   We have no strong opinion as to who should have the responsibility for appointing these project officers, although in view of their immense fund of knowledge and their statutory duty to advise the public on matters relating to trees, it would perhaps lie most appropriately with the Forestry Commission. We did find, however, worrying indications of a rather narrow view of woodland management held by some of the Commission's present staff. The woodland project officers would need to acquire or be able to appreciate a wide range of skills and views of other disciplines (we hasten to add that the reverse is also true) similar to that undergone by our research team undertaking this study. Therefore special training might be needed.

3.10   From this need to balance sensitive woodland management with a variety of conservation constraints, there may be a case for the project officers to be appointed by the local authority in some counties. Many counties, through their detailed knowledge of local conditions and their planning work, have successfully developed policies which encompass rural industrial development and conservation. In a number of counties, too, it is the foresters in the countryside section of the planning department who have taken the initiative, and, although attitudes vary sharply between the study areas, in some a significant, cordial relationship has been built up between the local authority foresters and farmers and landowners. It may therefore be worthwhile, as an experiment, to split project officer appointments between the Forestry Commission and local authorities.

3.11   It has also been suggested that the work should be taken on by the Ministry of Agriculture, Fisheries and Food's Agricultural Development and Advisory Service (ADAS). It has a strong regional structure and an excellent relationship with farmers and landowners. The project officer role, perhaps as 'farm woodland adviser' could match up with the responsibilities for conservation generally which, for example, the Strutt Committee has recommended for ADAS [1].

3.12   The appointment of such officers would cost the taxpayer money, but we feel it would be in the nature of 'pump priming', and the release of resources now locked up in unused woodland would more than repay the investment.

Other Approaches

3.13   The appointment of project officers to be 'farmers' friends' may seem to further institutionalise a countryside possibly already overburdened in this direction, but with wit and sympathy this need not be so. In any case there is a great deal of room for enterprise in tackling neglected woodlands. Indeed, for the problems of 'valueless' woods and the uncertain markets noted earlier, some alternative approaches would be essential; there could also be problems with farmers who would be willing to see their woods worked over but who would not wish to take any personal interest or responsibility for the quality of work done. We suggest some alternative ways of dealing with such problems below.

3.14   Where woods are important for landscape or other considerations, there may be scope for the local authority to take them over, perhaps for a peppercorn rent, as has been the practice in Derbyshire for the last five years. In other cases the Woodland Trust may be able to lease or buy them outright or, for woodlands with particular wildlife interest, the local County Trust for Nature Conservation may have sufficient resources to be able to help manage them or take them over altogether, perhaps with the aid of the British Trust for Conservation Volunteers.

3.15   For the more valuable (timber) woodlands there would be a reasonable chance for the involvement of schemes run by consultancies which offer varying combinations of profit-sharing and rent, but these normally are only able to work with fairly large woods. There is also an embryonic interest by non farmers in 'hobby forestry' where a piece of woodland is managed for pleasure (as instanced by the Cambridgeshire owner quoted in paragraph 5.36). On a simpler level, we found some farmers to be interested in an *ad hoc* agreement to allow an owner of a woodburning stove to cut firewood: this could be an extremely useful and easy way of keeping some small woods open, particularly the many small alder and birch clumps on wet patches.

3.16   There is also considerable scope for two kinds of co-operative effort. First there is a number of examples in England and Wales of woodland co-operatives owned and operated by farmers for their own benefit. Second, there are possibilities for 'user co-operatives', such as the firewood co-operative now being formed to take the wood-burning stove idea mentioned above to its logical conclusion: a number of householders in South Devon have got together to lease enough woodland not only to keep them supplied with fuel on a sustained yield basis— but also to give them a guaranteed picnic spot (and adventure playground for their children).

3.17　But for areas like that studied in Cornwall something more systematic and larger in scale would be needed; here the need is greater and implies an altruism beyond that of enlightened self interest. One solution we favour is a publicly financed initiative on the lines of the Manpower Services Commission's 'Training Workshops' or Project Based Work Experience programmes using unemployed people to work in woods as part of a well-structured training scheme. We understand from the Chairman of the Forestry Training Council there is a shortage of skilled labour for forestry and harvesting contracting in some areas, of which Cornwall is one (paragraph C.9, Appendix II). Also, the present training facilities in the industry are heavily over-subscribed, with a long waiting list for forestry schools. It would seem sensible to put this regional need to good use in training woodmen for whom there would be a strong possibility of employment or self-employment once they had developed the necessary skills. If run in parallel with a project officer approach, such a scheme could be quite practical. Although the farmers concerned would be getting something for nothing, this does not seem to us to be an important objection—especially with woods whose speed of growth means that the present owners may not see any benefit in their lifetime.

Action

Grant Aid

3.18　There are a considerable number of bodies with responsibilities or strong interests in woodlands. Before we discuss the action required and who should do it, we would like to comment again on the present system of grant aid. We feel that it is far too inflexible. It takes no account of the existing condition of woodland and the vastly differing costs of putting matters right. The Forestry Commission's small woods grants are slightly higher for woods of less than three hectares but, as Table 5 (page 40) makes clear, this does not fully take into account the extra costs for a given area inevitable with the smallest woods. There are also the problems which arise when an owner wishes to manage woods for objectives which do not include timber. There is the prohibition on 'topping up' one grant with another, and there is the lack of grants for continuous systems of management.

3.19　We recommend that existing methods of grant aid should be reviewed against the objectives of the Department of the Environment's conservation and rural development policies. We suggest that it would be better to move towards the Countryside Commission's more flexible system of grant aiding in proportion to the cost of approved works; here the proportion of grant allowed is varied according to the landscape or other aims of each scheme, and the means used to achieve it. Over the years that the Countryside Commission have been aiding amenity tree planting schemes, they have satisfied themselves that this approach is perfectly manageable and have built in the necessary safeguards. There is no reason why this system should not be applied to woods over $\frac{1}{4}$-hectare. Also, the division of responsibility for grant aid between the Forestry Commission and the Countryside Commission should not be based on the size of the wood but on its primary management objective.

Strategy

3.20　**Countryside Commission.** Other than these changes to the system of grant aid, we recommend that the Countryside Commission should discuss with the Forestry Commission and the Nature Conservancy Council the joint funding of project officers: there are many ends to which woodland management may be directed, and a system of inter-agency co-operation stronger than the present simple consultation procedures needs to be set up. The Countryside Commission should also review their management agreements policy in the light of this report; if project officers are appointed to specific countryside areas, then there may be opportunities to arrange simultaneous agreements on landscape management and public access for several holdings. They should also consider how restoring and improving woodlands might fit more effectively into their current new agricultural landscapes work.

3.21　**Forestry Commission.** The Forestry Commission have already taken some action in relation to small woodlands on farms: a project officer has been seconded to work in the Gwent study area. Also, some of their district officers are experimenting with alternative woodland management systems; their Research Branch is developing its native broadleaved tree seed sources for the nursery trade; and their Private Forestry and Land Use Planning Branch is collecting information on the implications for local employment of home-grown hardwood timber from small woods. Apart from making wider use of project officers in specific areas, which at the moment the Commission are unable to do, there is little to add except that we suggest that they should include in their in-service training schemes greater consideration of the multi-purpose management of small woods.

3.22 **Ministry of Agriculture, Fisheries and Food.** As well as adopting the project officer approach, the Ministry of Agriculture, Fisheries and Food, through ADAS, could play a key role as disseminators of advice, information and ideas about the future of woods. Their Land Service officers have some forestry training and, without necessarily forcing the pace, could, where the circumstances warrant it, encourage farmers and landowners to spend time or money or both on woods, and persuade them that such action is in the best interests of good husbandry and effective land management. They also have a useful contact role and can, in consultation with other appropriate bodies, ensure that the plans and practices put forward for land management are feasible and practical within each farmer's or landowner's individual circumstances (perhaps encouraging the farm forestry speculated on in paragraph 6.21). As an extra or marginal enterprise such woodland management would be of interest also to ADAS socio-economic advisers.

3.23 **Development Commission.** Earlier we suggested that putting the rehabilitation of small woods on a long-term basis would require inputs of management and investment from the home-grown timber trade. Assistance towards this would be the responsibility of the Development Commission, mainly through their agency, CoSIRA. In Wales, this responsibility now rests with the Welsh Development Agency.

3.24 **Nature Conservancy Council.** The Nature Conservancy Council has laid great stress on the value, mainly for scientific reasons, of ancient woodlands. Each wood is more or less unique, and the advice of the Council's officers would frequently be needed to give a view on the nature of woodland and its potential for conservation, and to advise on certain aspects of management.

3.25 **Manpower Services Commission.** The Manpower Services Commission could help small woods through the sort of training workshop or project suggested in paragraph 3.17. Such a programme would need to be sustained not for just two or three years but for decades, so as to have a realistic chance of becoming self-financing as woodlands are progressively improved.

3.26 **Local Authorities.** Local authorities have wide planning responsibilities and most have the kind of experience to provide a degree of balance to the enthusiasm of the specialists and to take the long view regarding their districts' or counties' environments and economies. They might also play the more positive role suggested in paragraph 3.10 by appointing project officers or, more simply, by ensuring that advice is available in areas not covered by project officers.

3.27 **Other Organisations.** Private consultants and a number of voluntary organisations have a major part to play, as do the Royal Institution of Chartered Surveyors and the Farming and Wildlife Advisory Groups. The importance of forestry to the Royal Institution of Chartered Surveyors is reflected in the written and practical examinations for its Land Agency and Agriculture Division, whose members advise landowners and farmers on the management of a large number of often extensive estate woodlands. The Institution may wish to consider the need for special advice from its members directed more towards the long-term future of small woods as well as their potential role in the key question of marketing. Farming and Wildlife Advisory Groups are already active in a number of counties. Their members, wearing other hats, tend to be officers of several organisations already mentioned. But the Groups' interests overlap heavily with the recommendations of this report, and to date two counties have full-time advisers on an experimental basis who are already proving to be most helpful by offering advice and making new contacts among farmers. Their role could be widened to promote greater awareness of and action to help small woodlands.

Figure 2
Areas of Woodland* Summary
Shown by percentage

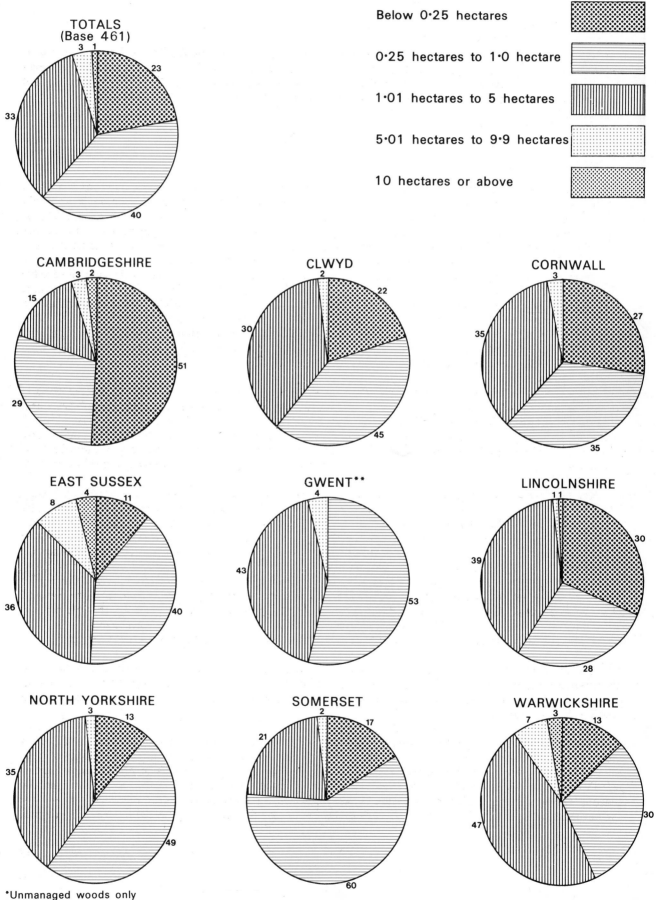

Below 0·25 hectares

0·25 hectares to 1·0 hectare

1·01 hectares to 5 hectares

5·01 hectares to 9·9 hectares

10 hectares or above

TOTALS
(Base 461)

CAMBRIDGESHIRE

CLWYD

CORNWALL

EAST SUSSEX

GWENT**

LINCOLNSHIRE

NORTH YORKSHIRE

SOMERSET

WARWICKSHIRE

*Unmanaged woods only

**Woods less than 0·25 ha were not surveyed in the Gwent pilot study

4   Landscape, Wildlife and Historical Heritage

Appraisal

4.1   **Before going into details it may be helpful to define the types of woodland studied. Although there is enormous variation in the origin, size, species composition, management (both past and present) and condition of small woodlands, it is possible to categorise generally the types of woods surveyed to reflect their present physical character and condition. Their contribution to landscape, wildlife conservation and historical heritage is then considered.**

Woodland Types

4.2   Figures 2 and 3 bring together the data on areas and types of woodland. No upper size limit was placed on the woods surveyed, but woods over ten hectares were infrequent. In principle, the Forestry Commission would consider entering into a Basis III Dedication Agreement with the owner of woods of more than ten hectares. This is significant in that there is a presumption that dedicated woodland is managed primarily for timber production, and to a plan of operations consistent with "... sound forestry practice; but with the additional objectives of effective integration with agriculture, environmental safeguards, and such opportunities for recreation as may be appropriate" [21]. With dedication, commercial criteria (such as net discounted revenue and internal rate of return) are normally used to formulate a plan of operations. Woods of less than ten hectares are not accepted in the scheme as they are not usually considered 'economically viable'. This over-simplifies the position, but, although the Forestry Commission treat individual applications on merit (as when two or more woods together measure ten hectares or more), it is a widely accepted rule of thumb. Thus only a small proportion of the woods surveyed might, on the face of it, justify investment with the primary objective of a commercially judged return.

4.3   At the other end of the scale, only one-fifth of the woods surveyed covered less than 0.25 hectare, the size which normally makes a wood eligible for grant from the Countryside Commission for amenity planting and management. (This again over-simplifies the situation in that, where the owner's proposals cannot be admitted by the Forestry Commission because they are designed specifically for amenity purposes, then application may be made to the Countryside Commission). Locally, however, these very small woodlands may be quite frequent —as in Cambridgeshire and Lincolnshire; and their importance in the landscape is not to be judged by their size.

4.4   Overall, about three-quarters of the woods surveyed covered between 0.25 and ten hectares, and would fall within the Forestry Commission's Small Woods Scheme. As with dedication, the primary objective must be timber production, although amenity and conservation are also likely to be (but are not necessarily) important objectives: "Special emphasis will be given to the planting of broadleaves where sites are suitable and where the existing landscape is essentially broadleaved in character ... in many lowland areas there will be a presumption in favour of grant-aiding broadleaved planting under the scheme" [21]. These grants are normally for planting and establishing new woods, and although applications for improving existing woods by selective planting or natural regeneration are considered, they are not normally eligible for grant unless there is a convincing amount of existing natural regeneration or unless the amount of planting is proportionately great. (In this last case the grant is based on the area planted, not the area of the wood. Thus woods to be managed primarily for landscape and wildlife conservation are not eligible, nor are many possible approaches to restoring woodlands).

4.5   Figure 3 summarises the type of woodlands—their present physical character and condition. We have divided them into eleven categories which can be linked one to another in terms of their relationship and in terms of the changes or developments which we found occurring in the study areas. Figure 4 represents these relationships diagrammatically.

4.6   **Category A** (recently planted woodland) is composed mostly of woods we have called 'managed', which are a matter for concern only insofar as felling and other operations prior to replanting, or the species of trees planted, have impacts on the landscape or wildlife etc. In general we regard it as reassuring that an average of one in ten woods were found to have been extensively or completely replanted, since, no matter what the reasons, this is a strong indication of farmers' and landowners' interest in the continuation of their woods. However, as is discussed below, in a number of cases the wrong thing may have been done for the right reasons.

Figure 3
Types of Woodland* Summary
Shown by percentage

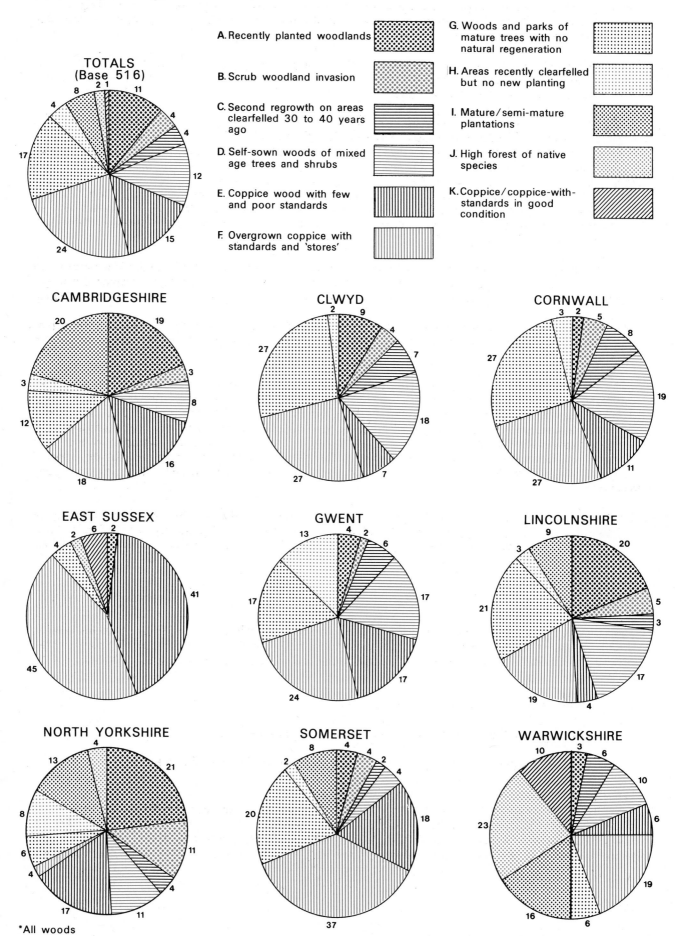

A. Recently planted woodlands

B. Scrub woodland invasion

C. Second regrowth on areas clearfelled 30 to 40 years ago

D. Self-sown woods of mixed age trees and shrubs

E. Coppice wood with few and poor standards

F. Overgrown coppice with standards and 'stores'

G. Woods and parks of mature trees with no natural regeneration

H. Areas recently clearfelled but no new planting

I. Mature/semi-mature plantations

J. High forest of native species

K. Coppice/coppice-with-standards in good condition

TOTALS
(Base 516)

CAMBRIDGESHIRE

CLWYD

CORNWALL

EAST SUSSEX

GWENT

LINCOLNSHIRE

NORTH YORKSHIRE

SOMERSET

WARWICKSHIRE

*All woods

4.7   **Category B** (scrub woodland) and **Category C** (secondary regrowth) are stages in parallel processes. Scrub woodland is mainly the invasion of neglected agricultural land by 'pioneer' species of trees and shrubs—usually hawthorn, blackthorn, birch and alder (depending on site conditions). Secondary regrowth is the (mainly non-coppice) regrowth of woodland clearfelled thirty to forty years ago. However, because of differing soil and micro-climate conditions on old woodland sites, and the likelihood of shrubs and ground vegetation surviving clear felling operations, Category C is usually botanically richer than Category B.

4.8   **Category D** (self sown woods) is the result of the evolution of Categories B and C over a period of time. It consists of trees and shrubs of mixed ages, and is the most natural looking woodland in the study areas, with many species and a wide distribution of age classes.

4.9   **Category E** (coppice wood with few and poor standards) and **Category F** (over-grown coppice with standards and stores) represents two conditions of coppice. Category E occurs mainly where an even-aged crop of standards has been removed from over hazel coppice and a hawthorn understorey. The stumps of the timber trees are too old to coppice and, as the uncut hazel and thorn cannot grow into trees to take their place, they form a tangle of vegetation which inhibits any seedling invasion from outside. A sprinkling of poor standards unwanted by timber merchants remains. Category F differs in that the cut stumps can still support coppice regrowth, or the coppice understorey is composed of species (such as ash, beech, elm, lime, oak, sweet chestnut) which are capable of growing on into full sized trees. If the stems are singled and thinned then they will eventually grow into Category I or J, depending on the range of species.

4.10   **Category G** consists of woods more appropriately described as wood-pasture. Similar in appearance to old parkland with rather isolated trees in a sward regularly grazed by livestock, so keeping down any regeneration, they are of an age when they are unlikely to give rise to any coppice regeneration after clearfelling.

4.11   **Category H** is woods which have been recently clearfelled (they may well still be shown on the map as woods) but where there is no clear indication of their future development either naturally or by human intervention.

4.12   **Categories I** (mature or semi-mature plantations) **J** (high forest of mainly native species) and **K** (coppice or coppice with standards in good condition) are also 'managed' woodlands in the sense that they represent woodland conditions desired by forest managers for the production of different forest products. Category I may have an admixture of natural regeneration and coppice, and Category J may have a few planted exotics. They may have reached this stage of development more by accident than design, but that does not mean that they are less satisfactory than woods managed more purposefully. This satisfaction may, however, be tempered by the extent to which there are implications for landscape and wildlife conservation if they are not properly managed in the future.

4.13   Generally speaking, Category C approximates to the ecologists ideal high forest with a wide range of species and forms, fairly high light intensities and frequent open spaces, whilst Category J approximates to the foresters ideal of few species, good form, high stocking density and (in a large wood) a good distribution of age classes.

Landscape Values

4.14   How important small woodlands are to the landscapes of the study areas cannot be assessed objectively, since landscape is a human concept and is subject to the perceptions and prejudices both of the writers and the readers of this report. We have, however, posed ourselves three questions about the small woodlands in the study areas:

    i.   Who sees them in the course of a year?

    ii.   Would it matter to those who saw them if they disappeared?

    iii.   How do we as research consultants feel about the landscape of the areas studied?

Who Sees Them?

4.15   There are three broad groups of people to whom the woods are at least periodically visible: farmers and owners who live amongst them; people who live in nearby towns and villages from which they are visible; and visitors who see them in the course of their journey or (in much smaller woods) who stay within the areas. The views of farmers and landowners are explored in Chapter 6, but it can be said that the overwhelming majority

Figure 4
Changes taking place in woodland in the study areas

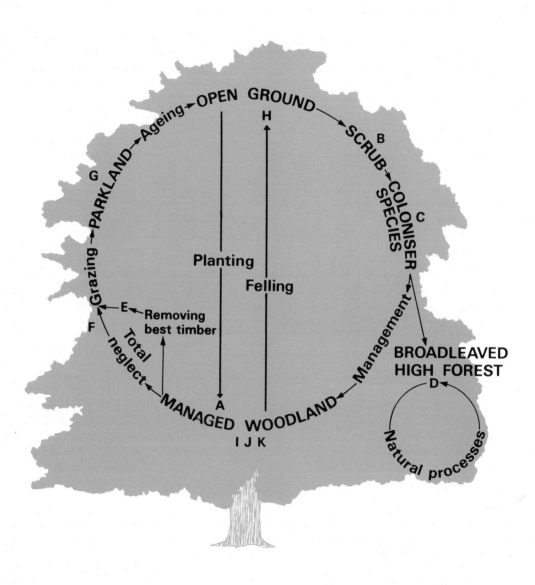

Within the diagram:

OPEN GROUND

Ageing → PARKLAND → Grazing

SCRUB → COLONISER SPECIES

Planting

Felling

Removing best timber

Total neglect

Management

BROADLEAVED HIGH FOREST

Natural processes

MANAGED WOODLAND

I J K

A — Recently planted woodlands

B — Scrub woodland invasion

C — Secondary regrowth on areas clearfelled 30 to 40 years ago

D — Self-sown woods of mixed age trees and shrubs

E — Coppice wood with few and poor standards

F — Overgrown coppice with standards and 'stores'

G — Woods and parks of mature trees with no natural regeneration

H — Areas recently clearfelled but no new planting

I — Mature/semi-mature plantations (may have admixture of natural regeneration and coppice)

J — High forest of native spp. (may have a few planted exotics)

K — Coppice/coppice-with-standards in good condition

of those interviewed have at least some awareness of the small woodlands around them, and a fair proportion are strongly aware of their presence. Woods are thought to be important to the landscape (though the ones on their own farms are not necessarily appreciated in the same way), and concern at their disappearance was frequently expressed, with a significant number mourning their loss.

4.16   The terms of reference did not include obtaining the views of those who live in or near the study areas but who do not take their livelihood from the land; however, there is evidence of local access to the countryside—in Clwyd, East Sussex and Warwickshire, for example—which implies enjoyment of the landscape. There is also the considerable number of visitors and long-distance travellers who can see woodland areas on their journeys, although this aspect varies from area to area, both in the numbers of travellers and in the quality of the landscape. The Cornwall study area, despite being in a location generally popular with tourists, can be seen only by those deliberately exploring the county's byways, and much the same applies to the Lincolnshire area. However, most of the study areas are on or highly visible from heavily used roads or tourist routes, and many recent surveys show that visitors to the countryside are appreciative of the part woodlands play in the scenery.

Would it Matter if they Disappeared?

4.17   The importance to 'outsiders' of small woodlands in the landscape probably lies less in their actual presence or absence than in the contribution they make to overall diversity in the scene. On the whole, diversified landscapes are more attractive than those featuring one dominant land use. Linton [42] puts areas containing at least two of the three major land uses—agriculture, moorland and woodland—in the highest but one category in terms of scenic attractiveness. Whether this follows from contemporary tastes [44] or from the need of the human eye for reference points [49], or from something more atavistic [3], does not seem to matter: the presence of small woods is noted (if only unconsciously) and their presence is valued. Thus, in most of the areas studied, if the woods disappeared altogether they would be missed by a large number of people. Of course, as the maps in each case study report show (Appendix II), not all small woodlands are of equal landscape importance; indeed, there are many whose absence would be noted by only a few local people, mainly farmers and landowners and their families. Depending on one's viewpoint, this may suggest (alarmingly to some) that farmers or landowners could remove woods and that nobody would notice that they had gone, or (reassuringly to others) that landscape constraints are not absolute and that there is flexibility for development in land management.

4.18   The above argument begs the question of the contribution made by small woods to landscape quality— for example, the contrasts between the often rounded margins of long-established woods of mainly broadleaved species, the more angular appearance of many conifer woods, and the chequered effect of new plantations of any species. There is also the question of woods which look similar from the outside but inside offer different experiences to the walker or rider.

The Consultants' View

4.19   On these questions we must express our personal opinion. For several months, in autumn, winter and spring, in good and bad weather, we did not just 'see' the woods in the study areas, together with the surrounding landscape, we *looked* at them and made an appraisal of them. Cambridgeshire and North Yorkshire excepted, there appears to be a certain 'rightness' to the woodland landscape. The woods are normally on land which has not in the past been very useful for agriculture—the steeper slopes, the scarp quarries, the boggy hollows and streams—and thus appears to be integral with both the differing topography and agriculture of each area. Where their location makes it more obvious that they have been planted and are not 'natural', such as on hilltops and along roads, they serve usually to accentuate topographical features. Where planted for game or amenity purposes, their appearance in the landscape is less 'organic' but still functional. (The invasion by scrub of neglected farmland in Gwent was something of an affront to the eye.)

4.20   With this order comes welcome changes in colours and textures from those of the agricultural activities around them—true both of summer and winter. Any variation in height from the fields around gives great visual appeal especially in the flatter areas of Cambridgeshire, Lincolnshire and Warwickshire. Contrasts with nearby less well wooded areas are often notable—as in Gwent and Somerset, for example. On the often vexed question of conifers, we noted with pleasure the frequent leavening of green in the predominantly winter browns of the woods and the warm colour of Scots pine bark in the evening sunshine. However, stands of pure conifers seem less fitting, mainly because the species commonly found in the woods surveyed (pines, spruces, larches and firs) tent to lose their bottom branches in middle age and look leggy and somewhat bedraggled at the woodland edge. In general, the greater the range of species in a wood, the better it appears from the middle distance, because of the many-shaded effect produced, both in and out of leaf.

4.21   Middle-distance viewing of mainly broadleaved woods is deceptive, however, in that it is usually impossible to judge their internal condition. Woods can and do belie their healthy external appearances. Many woods, although apparently healthy and vigorous externally, have severe problems of neglect, decay or mismanagement when examined close at hand. It follows of course that woods in a satisfactory ecological or forestry condition can look equally attractive in the landscape as those in poor condition.

4.22   There are changes in the physical condition of woods which are having some visual impact in all areas except, perhaps, East Sussex. Foremost is the high death rate from Dutch elm disease, affecting every area except East Sussex and Lincolnshire, and particularly damaging to the woods in Cambridgeshire and Warwickshire. Because elm is such a tall tree, the dead stag heads are highly visible; moreover they will not become overgrown often until the crown rots or the tree falls. In Cambridgeshire elm is the dominant species in many small woods, and the disease has ravaged them, leaving only an understorey of hawthorn and elder. The Lincolnshire area, excepting a miracle, is bound to go the same way. Although neglect may have little direct visual impact on the outside observer, inside the woods is a different matter, and possibly even more a matter of taste than the exterior. A wildlife enthusiast or a gamekeeper may approve of a tangle of undergrowth, whilst a casual walker or a forester may not. A dark wood may trouble the eye but give easier passage on foot.

4.23   Immediately visible in the landscape are the sites of clearfelled and replanted, or newly established woods. These may be divided into three broad groups: pure or almost pure conifers, conifer and broadleaved mixtures, and hybrid poplars. Examples of the first were found in Cornwall (where the climate and soils grow excellent spruce and Douglas fir), Clwyd and North Yorkshire. Conifer and broadleaved mixtures were noted in East Sussex, Lincolnshire and Cambridgeshire, and hybrid poplar plantations in Clwyd, Warwickshire and Cambridgeshire. All have an immediate visual impact caused by the small size of the trees and the regularity of the rows in which they are planted. This cannot be avoided in the short term when normal methods of replanting are used. The longer term impact is less easy to judge, as both woods and opinions change over time, and subsequent management becomes a critical factor. If the management of mixed plantations favours the broadleaved trees, then the woods will gradually look more like the ones they have replaced. If not, then they may remain predominantly coniferous in character (which appears to have happened to earlier mixed plantations in North Yorkshire). If the poplar plantations are left unpruned (on the outside at least) and allowed to close their canopy, then the general character of the woods will be not dissimilar to woods of other broadleaved species. But if they are managed properly [26], then this will not happen and, like pure conifer plantations, they will look considerably different when compared to other broadleaved stands in most of the areas. Whether they will look better or worse is then a matter of personal opinion. (Our own view is that, in most areas, the character of the landscape is likely to change for the worse, with a significant reduction in the subtlety of colour and shape compared to mixed broadleaved woodlands.)

4.24   As mentioned earlier, the visual impact of mismanagement or abuse is less obvious, but it is there to be seen in most areas—notably in Clwyd, Gwent and North Yorkshire. It arises almost entirely from heavy grazing, and its most visible effect is a park-like quality with a light stocking of mature trees on a grassy sward. With smaller woods, this prevails throughout, but in larger woods it occurs mainly at the margins. The process is slow, but can be reversed by excluding stock for a few years. However, the grazing and shelter obtained may have long been a deliberate part of the farm's management, and therefore exclusion would be difficult. Its effects are very slow in woods where oak is the dominant species, such as in Cornwall, but can be relatively fast where there is birch and alder, for example in Gwent. The condition of the edges of woods grazed in this way is readily visible, but the *reduction* in area is not so noticeable—rather like the slow melting of a block of ice. It is only when map comparisons are possible that the real effect can be judged.

Wildlife Conservation

4.25   To appraise wildlife values is somewhat easier than to appraise the landscape, largely because there is a more scientific basis for assessment. The following is based, a little loosely, on conclusions reached by Peterken [58], [59], [60] and [61], Moore [50] and [52] and Tubbs [71]. As Peterken [60] points out: "Woodlands cover an ecological range which is almost as large as all other land uses and semi-natural vegetation types put together . . . All woodland contributes in some way to the objectives of nature conservation." This conservation value arises from three closely linked aspects:

    i.   woodlands as habitats in relation to the pattern of local land use;

    ii.   woodlands as representative examples of semi-natural ecosystems or habitats (now very scarce in Britain);

    iii.   woodlands as examples of man's impact on these semi-natural habitats.

Habitats and Local Land Use

4.26   The first of these relates mainly to existing woods in terms of their value to the fauna of the area. As the intensity of farming has grown, with simplified cropping systems demanding the removal of trees and hedges, the value of woods as undisturbed wildlife habitats has increased. As explained in Chapter 1, no systematic collection of data on birds, mammals, reptiles or insects was possible, so only very general remarks may be made. Nevertheless, it will be clear from the paragraphs on game conservation, that woods are a valuable habitat for breeding birds (and predators). Despite the fact that the study was done largely out of the breeding season, there was ample evidence of bird and animal life, much of which centred on the woods. Particularly obvious were the many badger holts, rookeries, duck and pheasant nests, and (less happily for farmers) rabbit warrens and pigeon's nests. Hares were also plentiful in the Lincolnshire and Cambridgeshire woods, and the presence of deer was noted by the game consultant in East Sussex and Warwickshire.

4.27   In absolute terms, the woodlands in the study areas may not have high values for fauna. As Moore and Hooper point out [51], farmland birds are essentially woodland species. And to double the number of species needs a tenfold increase in woodland area; so the bigger the wood the better. Nevertheless, all woods have some value for birds, and even quite small ones may support many of the common British species. In the Lincolnshire and Cambridgeshire study areas, small woods are now tiny islands in a sea of carefully drained, heavily cultivated farmland. It is not only the presence of trees and shrubs for shelter and nesting, but also the presence of ponds, streams and other wet areas within them which makes them so valuable.

Semi-natural Woodland

4.28   Peterken [60] and [61] lists five types of woodland which are of special scientific interest:

    i.   relics of the mediaeval wood-pasture system;

    ii.   ancient high forest woods with continuity from Boreal times;

    iii.   ancient coppice woodlands;

    iv.   ancient woods in inaccessible sites;

    v.   woods formed by at least 150 years of largely natural succession and structural development.

We judge that examples of (iii) are to be found in every area studied except, perhaps, Clwyd and North Yorkshire. Examples of (v) are probably present in East Sussex, Gwent, Lincolnshire and Somerset. The incidence of examples of (iv) is very hard to judge, but they may be present in the Cornwall and Gwent areas. The value of these woods lies partly in that they contain some of the last remaining examples of tree, shrub and ground plant species which are indigenous to these regions and which survive only in small fragments of the original woodland.

4.29   An analogy can be made between islands surrounded by water and these woodland habitat 'islands' within a matrix of other habitats. The number of wildlife species which a wood can hold in equilibrium depends on its area and isolation—larger woods tend to hold more than smaller ones; and not only true woodland species but also a range of other wildlife because of the greater frequency of clearings, rides and fringes. Although there are complexities of soil, micro-climate, extinction and invasion to consider, together with the use made of these 'island' woods by man which adds further complications, in general for a given area an isolated wood tends to hold fewer species than one closer to other woods. Again, for a given area, the older the wood the more plant species it is likely to have within it. All the study areas have woods which, as indicated by the number of plant species (together with other evidence such as sinuous or eccentric boundaries), are of great age. Also, due to the 'island' nature of their habitats, many of these plants may not be found anywhere else in the area, and therefore will be lost if such woods are not conserved.

4.30   This is taken a step further by Peterken *et al*, who demonstrate the value of woods (with other relict features) as 'gene pools'—archives or banks where plants of wide genetic diversity are stored (particularly tree and grass species). Besides being of great interest in themselves they are 'controls' which can be used to compare what is happening to the genetic make-up of the vegetation in the matrix of land around these woods; and they are a breeding stock against a future need. In an uncertain age, it would be foolish to ignore the value for this purpose of many of the woods studied (and, by extension, others in their vicinity).

4.31   However, these are two rather narrow facets of the value of woods as habitats, and as examples of man's impact on them. Habitats are associations of species of plants and animals and are the medium within which most species perpetuate themselves. It is impossible, outside controlled climate conditions in the laboratory, to select some species as rare or useful and thus to be conserved whilst others are written off. The whole is needed to maintain any chosen part. Woods contain (and are themselves) mosaics of vegetation which influence the soil and the micro-climate in a self-perpetuating way. These mosaics support animal life and are the principal basis of the ecosystem of their area—remove them and the consequent effects ripple outwards. These ecological conditions cannot be recreated if destroyed; if they could it would take millenia and presuppose the existence of other woodlands nearby to act as the source of transferable plant and animal material.

4.32   Ancient woodland is unique in its ecological make-up. As a source of study for investigating man's effect on the environment a considerable number of such woods are needed to establish parameters. It follows that the removal or radical treatment of even one of these old woods diminishes the value of all for scientific purposes. It was not within the remit of this study to quantify accurately the proportion of ancient woods, but the ratio is certainly highly significant, and we consider their value for wildlife conservation (in its widest sense) to be high.

Man's Impact

4.33   Such values are, of course, subject to change. Even if carefully managed for conservation, small fragments of larger woods will tend to lose some of their initially high population of vascular plants and associated species. They will also tend to be invaded by other species from the surrounding country. This is normal and is itself a substantial field for study. However, there are other factors noted during the study and referred to elsewhere which give rise to concern: These are:

     i.   woodland clearance, for agriculture or for re-afforestation;

     ii.   the effects of continuous (and, sometimes, long-established) grazing;

     iii.   the effects of neglect.

4.34   **Woodland Clearance.** Total clearance of woodland for agriculture is self-evidently destructive of wildlife habitats. Total or substantial clearance for re-afforestation can be less damaging in the short term, but in the medium term it can be very destructive, as Peterken [60] makes plain: ". . . even long-established woods are habitually reduced to 'bare ground' before British foresters regard them as ready for proper management." The whole micro-climate is suddenly altered and only gradually (with the growth of the newly planted trees) moves back towards what is normal in woodlands. To the shock caused by this suddenly brighter and colder environment is then added the almost explosive growth of some plant species (particularly brambles, bracken and grasses), coupled with invasion of other species from the surrounding area. Initially this may result in a wider range of plant species than were present before, but some susceptible (and often rare and highly specialised) species will have been extinguished. A number of the newly cleared and replanted woods in the survey has been neglected and the new trees have not survived, so there is not even the satisfaction of continued woodland cover. We have two particular examples in mind—'plantations' in Somerset and Lincolnshire which are so thick with brambles and hawthorn that they are almost impossible to penetrate. They will eventually revert to woodland, but are examples of bad conservation and silvicultural practice and so are a waste of resources.

4.35   Where the planted trees thrive, however, there are then consequential ground and soil effects as they close the canopy, since (poplars excepted) they cast a heavy shade. This process happens both with coniferous and broadleaved trees, due usually to the high density of planting. In the long term, as thinning takes place and mature trees are removed, the process is reversed to some extent [56], but this pre-supposes a reservoir of survivor plants from which re-colonisation can take place, and even then it may not happen since the ability of many plant species to recolonise is extremely low. In any event, some species will probably be lost. Poplars are rather different in that, properly planted and managed, the canopy never closes; the foliage is fairly fine, and light intensities approach those of more diverse semi-natural woodland. Therefore the micro-climate is more favourable to the conservation of the existing ground flora than in conventional plantations. But the initial shock of clearance remains, and plant diversity is diminished by the removal of the original tree species.

4.36   One cannot be dogmatic about the survival of ground flora under different kinds of management, since it varies enormously from east to west Britain. In the milder, moister climate of the west, typical woodland plants such as bluebells and primroses can stand considerable exposure and still thrive, whereas in the eastern counties drought or frost would destroy them once tree cover was removed.

4.37   The last point in the preceding paragraph underlies the concern ecologists show at the replacement of native trees with exotics. This is not xenophobia but rests on the knowledge that native trees support a much greater range and number of parasites and invertebrates than introduced species. Replacing them with exotics depletes the food chain accordingly. Many invertebrates, for instance, are able to feed only on one species of plant, and an English oak may support over 300 species of insect, compared to only about seven on sycamore. The consequences for birdlife, for example, are obvious.

4.38   In the North Yorkshire study area, where woods have been cleared and replanted, the original woods also appear to have been plantations, with a high incidence of non-native species such as sycamore and larch. In this area, therefore, clearance and replanting with conifers or a conifer and broadleaved mixture would be less damaging. Elsewhere, and despite the clear sympathy for the environment apparent in, for example, one area in Clwyd, the end result of replanting is likely to be an impoverished botanical heritage—a scientific fact, expressed without emotion.

4.39   **Grazing.** The effects of grazing are more immediately evident and more straightforward to appraise. Grazing animals (and particularly sheep) on a semi-continuous basis depletes the ground and shrub flora both directly by damage from grazing and browsing, and indirectly by compacting the soil. The policy followed by some farmers in Somerset, Cornwall, Clwyd and North Yorkshire is to turn their livestock into the woods in wet weather to avoid sward damage to their fields. This could be particularly damaging to the woodland flora and soil locally and if carried on over a period of decades it will first deplete and then eventually kill the woodland itself.

4.40   There is nothing new in this. The mediaeval Cistercian monks in Yorkshire systematised the process by using goats followed by sheep to clear the primary woodland [39]. Farmers in Gwent who have up to 25 per cent of their holding as woodland are understandably keen on reclaiming some of it in this inexpensive way. But a number of farmers are unaware of the implications of what they are doing. Only in the more arable study areas of Cambridgeshire and Lincolnshire (and to a lesser extent in East Sussex) is this process not at work. The effects of unringed pigs kept in a small wood in the Somerset study area are dramatic—the earth is totally bare throughout.

4.41   **Neglect.** The results of neglect in the woods we surveyed are more subtle than either clearance or grazing. Reference to Figure 3 and paragraphs 4.6 to 4.12 will show that categories C, D, I, J and K constitute only 25 per cent of total woodlands. These are the categories where the woodland is either reasonably 'natural' (C and D) or held in a state favourable to wildlife by sympathetic management (including cases, such as in Warwickshire where lack of management has fortuitously led to that condition) (I, J and K).

4.42   A fallacy we found to be widely held by those with an interest in wildlife but little technical or scientific knowledge of woodlands is that the habitat value of a wood is maintained or enhanced by leaving it completely alone. It is true that this is a better conservation practice than abusing it or doing the wrong thing, but it indicates a misunderstanding of the dynamic nature of woodland conditions. Left to themselves, categories B and C woods would evolve into category D which, in its diversity of species and ages, is—broadly speaking—self-perpetuating and ecologically satisfactory. However, B might in fact have been more valuable for the plant communities found in its permanent pasture than under the closed canopy of the main pioneer tree species—usually birch and alder in the areas studied. Both B and C will tend to close canopy for a period of decades until windblow, disease and old age give rise to a more varied structure. Thus, strictly, only category C (roughly equivalent to Peterken's Type v—paragraph 4.28 above) would benefit from a policy of benign neglect. All other categories require management in order to conserve or enhance their wildlife values.

4.43   It is quite clear from research done over the last three decades and reported by all the scientists referred to in this chapter that there are no woods or forests in Great Britain which have not been modified by man's past activities—hence the use of the term 'semi-natural'. Add to this the facts that a wood's habitat value increases with its age, and that the relics of ancient woodland usually contain the richest plant communities, including the rarer species, and it is then apparent that woodland wildlife has evolved from its original wildwood nature to match the conditions created and altered by man's actions or 'management' over many centuries. This is what Peterken calls 'past-naturalness' [60] and it follows that continued management is needed to maintain this valued condition.

4.44   Therefore, from Figure 2, only 12 per cent of the woods (category D) could be left, with reasonable confidence, to fend for themselves (perhaps 16 per cent if caregory C is included); and another 9 per cent (categories I, J and K) are at present in a condition at least reasonably satisfactory for wildlife. A further 11 per cent had recently been planted (category A) and were thus regarded as being positively managed, whilst the 17 per cent in category G owe their condition mainly to grazing. The value for wildlife of the remaining 47 per cent has been impaired or is threatened by neglect. This is partly a matter of shade. In categories E and F, the cessation of felling, coppicing or both has resulted in a closed canopy—perhaps for the first time in centuries—and the resultant heavy shade has, in varying degrees, affected the ground vegetation. This is least noticeable in Cornwall, where the cover is predominantly oak, and most noticeable in East Sussex, where the hornbeam coppice casts a dense shade, although, this may not be too serious in its effects.

4.45 More serious is the reduction in management options (for wildlife among other objectives). Almost all the woods have been managed previously as coppice-with-standards. Coppice systems depend on reproduction by stool shoots or suckers. When they are felled at or near ground level, most broadleaved species—up to a certain age—reproduce from shoots sent up after cutting back to the stool or stump. These shoots arise either from dormant buds situated on the side of the stool at ground level, or from adventitious buds arising from the cambial layer round the periphery of the cut surface. Most species do not coppice from stools of large size, and it is usually necessary to fell trees when they are not more than forty years old, and sometimes when they are considerably younger [70]. Managed properly, coppice stools will live to a great age (by human standards they may be almost immortal [63]).

4.46 If coppice stools are not cut back in good time, then the bush or tree reverts to the life cycle normal for the species (with the interesting paradox noted by Rackham [63] that the better the soil and site conditions, the shorter the life). Therefore, once beyond the coppice stage, a wood—particularly in category G—must be managed either as high forest, or be carefully replanted with coppicing species. It is possible that an ancient wood would then have both its structure and species composition quite changed. Most of the woods surveyed which show this problem can still be brought back under some form of coppice management if their wildlife value (and the dependence of that value on continued coppice management) indicates it. But since so much of the growth dates back to World War II, work will need to be put in train soon if this management option is to be retained.

Historical Aspects

4.47 Since the historical aspects of small woods were not within the remit of the study, no data was gathered on which to base an appraisal. On the limited reading undertaken, the historical arguments for woodland conservation appear to relate to three aspects of woodlands: their links with the 'wildwood', as Rackham [63] and Edlin [17] call the prehistoric forests of Britain, their links with mediaeval and later rural economies, and the presence of archaeological features within them. There are biological dimensions to the first which we discuss in paragraphs 4.28 to 4.32, but on the geography of the wildwood this study is not competent to comment. Only in East Sussex is there clear evidence of any relationship with the local economy—that associated with the Wealden ironmasters. There are indications of boundary and other earthworks in a number of counties—notably Cambridgeshire, Lincolnshire and Warwickshire. Some of these are marked on the $2\frac{1}{2}$ inch Ordnance Survey maps but others are not. We made no systematic note of their presence. Rigg and furrow was also noticed in some woods in the same three counties.

4.48 It would appear, from our limited interpretation of the botanical and other evidence, that at least some of the woods are of considerable antiquity, and may be much altered remnants of the wildwood. If this is true, then they have an historical value of some importance. If it is not so, their age alone may still be such as to rank them with say, buildings surviving from the mediaeval period and, perhaps, equally worthy of conservation.

The Management Implications

4.49 **Although the ideal objectives of high landscape value and maximum nature conservation are different, it should be possible to reconcile most of the issues involved and manage woods in such a way as to achieve a high degree of compatibility between them. It is our view that the separate landscape, wildlife and historical conservation appraisals above have, to a considerable extent, similar implications for management.**

4.50 Peterken [61] has suggested some general principles on which woodland management for a number of objectives can be based. For the areas studied, the following guidelines could apply both to landscape and wildlife conservation objectives. They involve:

    i.   distinguishing between individual woods of high conservation value, areas rich in woodland of high conservation value, and other woodlands (the landscape analysis and vascular plant score maps in Appendix II show these separate aspects quite clearly);

    ii.   giving special treatment to special sites and areas by:

        a.   managing a proportion of woods on 'non-intervention' principles (eg category D woods);

b. maintaining or restoring traditional management where possible and appropriate (eg categories E, F and K);

c. where these options are not possible or appropriate, introducing alternative systems of management which retain or enhance the woods' conservation value (eg categories B, C and G);

iii. diminishing clearance—if no net reduction in the area of woodland is planned, then it is always better to keep existing woods rather than to create new ones;

iv. minimising rates of change within woods, giving particular attention to:

a. the distribution of broadleaf and conifer stands (for example, perpetuating existing broadleaved stands and confining conifers to where they are or have been growing);

b. the number and distribution of tree species, (keeping, where it is possible and economic to do so, the present mixture and avoiding monoculture);

c. the distribution of trees and stands of different ages to ensure there is always some tree cover;

d. carefully routeing roads, rides and paths to avoid ugly gashes in the canopy, reduce windblow, and conserve the diversity of vegetation.

v. encouraging some maturity by maintaining long rotations and retaining, for example, at least a scatter of old trees after restocking;

vi. replanting or encouraging the self-renewal of native tree species and using non-native species only when necessary or where long-established previously (as with the sycamore and conifer woods in the North Yorkshire study area);

vii. encouraging a diversity of woodland structure, tree and shrub species, and wildlife habitats (so far as this is compatible with other objectives).

4.51 A few simple examples may help to put this into perspective. In Cornwall the woods surveyed were mainly old oak coppice with standards. There are now no worthwhile markets for coppice oak, and the ground flora of these particular woods is probably not dependent on the retention of this system. A suitable approach would be to reduce the incidence of farm livestock grazing (say, for a decade in each area treated) in a systematic manner—working over most of the woods over a period of about fifty years. This could be coupled with group planting of oak of local strains in gaps and on pockets of deeper soil, which is sensible in forestry terms and goes some way to re-extending a genetic range depleted by perhaps a millenium of 'creaming off' the best formed trees.

4.52 In Somerset a similar approach to controlling grazing, coupled with sensible crown thinning of over-grown coppice, would be appropriate to the woods in the interior of the study area. For the more visible and larger scarp woods, a move towards continuous high forest management systems is indicated, probably with group felling and some group planting. The wetter areas of alder and ash could simply be left to themselves or could be periodically partially felled for firewood. In Gwent, there is a greater need for individual treatment and, because of the proximity of better markets, a wider range of options. The large scarp woods are of great landscape importance and there is a choice between coppice-with-standards and high forest systems; on balance, the latter course seems best suited to the ideals of both landscape and wildlife conservation. An 'irregular shelter-wood' [70] system or selection system would best maintain the exterior appearance of these woods but would favour shade-bearers, and a group system would probably be the best compromise—with group planting and some control of grazing. In the interior of the area there is scope for straight coppice systems (favouring the occasional standard) on a pulpwood rotation of twelve to fourteen years. Dingle and quarry woods could be fenced and left to themselves.

4.53 In the East Sussex area it would be a pity to miss the opportunity to bring back the former system of coppice-with-standards: hornbeam coppice managed on a fifteen to twenty year rotation for charcoal with some crown thinning and small group replanting of the standard oaks (ash regeneration can look after itself). In the present oak high forest, group felling is indicated, followed by natural regeneration if rabbits can be controlled effectively. The wetter ash and alder woods may be left or managed on a long rotation of, say, thirty years, for charcoal and firewood.

4.54   The Lincolnshire study area is more complex. There are wide variations in the historical and wildlife values of the woods, and landscape constraints are high, although one or two generalisations can be made. Woods which are manifestly old plantations now need crown thinning (to favour the ash rather than oak and sycamore). In the relict woods, a careful balance between crown thinning and group felling and planting is required. The open spaces noted in Appendix II need a cautious approach to determine how much should remain clear. Before planting, rabbit fencing and other forms of pest control should be tested to see if natural regeneration could be successful. (It is well to note that hares are numerous in this area, and are not kept out by rabbit fencing). Cricket bat willows (a variety of a native species) might well be tried in the many wet areas along the spring line. These areas are inconspicuously situated and already have alder present which would help reduce the visual impact of new willow plantations. With a number of woods having an open aspect, thickening their edges with suitable broadleaved species is necessary not only for landscape and wildlife reasons but also because most conifers fare badly on these dry soils or grow 'leggy'. Holly, thorn or wild rose or even evergreen oak could be used. There are also one or two woods which are both visually attractive and valuable for wildlife, but, because of the inherently poor soil conditions, they could simply be left alone to develop further from their present scrub thorn and elder status (perhaps with rabbit and hare control over small areas).

4.55   These approaches are also relevant to the Cambridgeshire area. But here more radical replanting is needed with the removal of dead elm, and underplanting with ash, oak and lime. A scattering of old standards should be left to maintain a degree of woodland micro-climate and continuity of the local species' genetic stock. In the North Yorkshire and Clwyd areas the former oak woods to the north and west respectively (which are now very open and with no regeneration) should ideally be completely replanted with oak. In the climate of these regions with their more exposed conditions, such plantings would need a nurse—possibly sycamore, which is tolerant of exposure, broadleaved and common elsewhere in the area. Livestock would obviously have to be fenced out. In the older plantations some crown thinning is needed together with the removal of suppressed trees. Because most of these plantations contain sycamore, the exclusion of livestock would give rise to rapid natural regeneration. In the larger and more conspicuous woods, this might also be achieved by group felling with the admixture of conifers where they existed before.

5   Forestry, Timber and Game

Appraisal

5.1   **These three aspects usually involve money in a much more direct way than landscape and wildlife and are therefore considered together in this chapter. The distinction between 'forestry' and 'timber' simply reflects the usual division between silviculture (the management of woods) and utilisation (the sale and use of woodland products). Evidence suggests that they are among the least appreciated and most undervalued of all the aspects examined in the course of this study.**

Forestry

5.2   Some of the elements and systems of forest management have already been referred to in Chapter 4, but a more direct appraisal is also needed. The majority of the woods surveyed show evidence of at least intermittent past management: the widespread incidence of beech and Scots pine well outside their original habitats [20], the presence of exotics such as sycamore, sweet chestnut, hybrid poplars, larch, and spruce, and the ubiquity of monoculture coppice (mostly hazel but also hornbeam and sweet chestnut) which is slow to spread naturally and much of which must have been planted. From the physical and verbal evidence little or no positive management has been carried out for at least forty years, and this neglect has been heavily compounded by the felling dictated by two World Wars. There are 'woods' (particularly in the Gwent, Somerset, and North Yorkshire areas), still shown as such on Ordnance Survey maps but which are now pasture or derelict gorse and bramble patches, totally devoid of the large oaks they once carried. Most woods with oak or ash standards suffered from heavy felling during the two Wars.

5.3   Partly because their size has made it uneconomic, and partly because (as discussed further in Chapter 6) there is no tradition of woodland management among farmers, a great many small woods have been left to their own devices. Their ability to recover from felling is dependent on their species composition and on other factors such as the incidence of stock grazing and rabbit control. In general, if grazing animals are excluded for a period, broadleaved species have the ability to restore woodland cover from reseeding and coppice. However, in some areas (notably those in Clwyd and North Yorkshire) oak seems less able than other species to regenerate itself, and could well become extinct as a woodland tree unless deliberately replanted or otherwise favoured.

5.4   It is accepted that woodlands which have been managed for a variety of forest produce, often for centuries [63], need bear little resemblance to the forester's ideal of a normal forest. Nevertheless, on turning a forester's 'eye for function' on the woods surveyed we were somewhat dismayed. Counting together categories A, I, J and K from Figure 2, only 20 per cent are in anything like a satisfactory condition (and some more by accident than design). To summarise, we found:

    i.   there is a high degree of dereliction, with:

        a.   poorly formed standards;

        b.   wild tangles of undergrowth;

        c.   heavily overgrown coppice unusable for its original purposes and most others;

    ii.   large areas of bare, or bramble and gorse-covered ground, often with stumps of old trees as mute testimony to the woods' former nature;

    iii.   low densities of trees of merchantable potential;

    iv.   unthinned maiden stems, and spindly and unstable stores;

    v.   poor age structure and a good deal of over-maturity;

    vi.   lack of regeneration caused by livestock or rabbits or hares, as well as damage by barking.

5.5   This general picture is made all the more depressing by an occasional wood which by receiving good management (or luck!) shows what potential many of these woods have for timber production. It was difficult to arrive at quantified assessments of this potential because it was not possible to find with sufficient accuracy the age of such trees or stands. This difficulty was compounded because the best trees had been creamed off, and one does not judge the potential yield from the poorer stems remaining. The following yield classes are estimated from height measurements and ring counts on felled trees or, in one or two cases, from the known date of felling or planting. They therefore should be viewed with caution although, except for those obtained from young plantations of known date, they are more likely to be under than over-estimates.

Table 2   Examples of Estimated Yield Classes in Small Woodlands—Summary Table

Study Area	Species	General Yield Class (in cubic metres per hectare per year)
Cambridgeshire	Oak (with European Larch nurse)	8
	Poplar	8,10
Gwent	Birch	12
Lincolnshire	Ash	6
	Elm	4
	European Larch	10
	Japanese Larch	12
	Scots Pine	8,14
North Yorkshire	Ash	6
	Sycamore	6
	European Larch	4
	Norway Spruce	6
Warwickshire	Oak	8
	Norway Spruce	16

5.6   The yield class is the maximum rate of growth of actual timber volume per year which could be obtained on that site; and 'general yield class' in Table 2 simply means that the figure has been obtained from the measured top height and age alone of the stand [24]. This is, broadly speaking, the estimated sustained yield under intensive management, and the figures indicate that growing conditions are near the middle of the range of variation in the North Yorkshire area and medium to good elsewhere. (A general yield class of 8 for oak puts it in the top growth bracket.) To achieve this in whole or in part is the proper function of good forest management, and it is worth noting here that it is foresters (and possibly only foresters) who have the necessary skills to achieve these production objectives in conjunction with the aims of landscape and wildlife conservation discussed in the previous chapter. They have the necessary techniques available to follow Peterken's fifteen principles [61], although it is fair to say that they would probably have to dig fairly deeply in their bag for the necessary but now long unused and old fashioned tools of management.

Timber

5.7   The quantities and values estimated for each area (unmanaged woodlands only) are summarised in Table 3.

Table 3   Quantities and Values of Forest Produce—Summary Table

Study Area (Unmanaged woodland area[1] in hectares)	Total Volume (cu. m[1])	Sawlogs Volume (cu. m[1])	Firewood (tonnes[1])	Pulpwood (tonnes[1])	Turnery wood (tonnes[1])	Charcoal (hectares[1])	Standing value (£)
Cambridgeshire (58)	11,644	6,799	7,444	—	—	—	180,392
Clwyd (39)	4.437	1,676	3,340	—	415[2]	—	34,048
Cornwall (62)	8,706	2,798	7,379	—	—	—	33,367
East Sussex (105)	12,480	5,488	3,042	—	—	92	267,220
Gwent (83)	5,760	2,188	2,636	3,141	—	—	45,782
Lincolnshire (100)	10,778	3,979	9,158	—	—	—	63,578

Table 3 Quantities and Values of Forest Produce—Summary Table—contd.

Study Area (Unmanaged woodland area[1] in hectares)	Total Volume (cu. m[1])	Sawlogs Volume (cu. m[1])	Other Produce				
			Firewood (tonnes[1])	Pulpwood (tonnes[1])	Turnery wood (tonnes[1])	Charcoal (hectares[1])	Standing value (£)
North Yorkshire (65)	4,691	1,833	3,746	—	—	—	27,373
Somerset (50)	7,812	7,867	5,843	—	—	—	56,091
Warwickshire (67)	7,149	3,210	3,457	—	1,257	—	130,928
Totals (629)	73,457[3]	35,838	46,045[4]	3,141	1,672	92	838,779

[1]Rounded to nearest whole number
[2]Includes 50 tonnes high quality Yew billets
[3]Total Volumes do not include branchwood
[4]Firewood tonnages include yield from branchwood

5.8   The valuations cover the 461 unmanaged woods (or parts of woods) which were surveyed. They are net values, being what a timber merchant or contractor might pay for the privilege of clearfelling the wood and disposing of its produce to the various markets available (plus a conservative addition, in more valuable woods, to include the element of increased value which normally results from 'felled measure'). They therefore take implicit account of the costs of felling, cleaning, causeway building, extraction to rideside, grading, loading, despatching, administration, and overheads; these can be very sizable items, even in large woods [31]. However, with small woods there are often considerable problems with the economy of scale: no less than 146 (32 per cent) of the woods surveyed and valued were judged to have no standing value at all. That is not to say they are entirely without value—for instance, the farmer or landowner using them as a source of domestic firewood would save the equivalent cost of other fuels—but it is unlikely that commercial buyers for forest produce would be found for them in the locality. These 'valueless' woods were distributed as shown in Table 4.

Table 4   Numbers of Woods Judged to have no Standing Value—Summary Table

	%			%
Cambridgeshire	28 (20)		Gwent	11 (8)
Clwyd	12 (8)		Lincolnshire	37 (24)
Cornwall	15 (10)		North Yorkshire	21 (14)
East Sussex	7 (5)		Somerset	8 (6)
			Warwickshire	7 (5)

5.9   The estimates of value also include a realistic reduction to take account of the difficulties of access. As noted in the case study reports (Appendix II), the majority of woods are on ground which is not suited to agriculture. Although some of the woods are level, dry, and lie handily at the sides of roads, others are on hilltops, on steep scarps, along streams, on boggy ground, or around old quarries and marlpits. Access is often difficult, through narrow farm gates, across fields, over streams or on terrain too steep for wheeled vehicles. There is a virtual certainty of at least minor damage to standing crops, soil structure, draining systems, gateways and so on. This aspect affects not only the values of forest produce but also the attitude of farmers towards harvesting it, and the seasonal timing of such operations.

5.10   There are two important points which arise from Tables 3 and 4: the extreme variation in values, and that they are quite high despite the difficulties referred to above. The variations are due partly to the intrinsic qualities of the woodlands: a good stand of oak, for instance, would attract buyers from anywhere in Great Britain. However, there is also a considerable variation in the regional markets for forest produce, and this should be examined in more detail: the markets for home-grown timber have to an extent not anticipated at the outset of this study become an important link in the chain of circumstances leading to the present state of small woodlands, and marketing is perhaps the most critical element in any proposal for improving them. The following examples illustrate the diversity of the present situation.

5.11 A small stand of fencing quality oak in the Cornwall study area had a standing value of less than half of an equivalent stand of oak in East Sussex or Lincolnshire. An accessible stand of reasonable sycamore had virtually no market value at all in Cornwall but had a value similar to beech (and not far short of fencing quality oak) in North Yorkshire. At the time of the survey, good quality poplar could be sold standing in East Sussex and Somerset but not in North Yorkshire and Clwyd; and, excepting pulp and turnery, there was almost no market at all for alder. For run-of-the-mill logs from woodland clearance, the influence of local specialist markets is significant: the price paid for hardwood pulp billets allowed a profit on cutting, loading, and transport costs in the Gwent area, but would result in a loss in the Lincolnshire area. Whole coppice woods were saleable standing for charcoal in East Sussex but not in any other study area. In general, for low quality woods and bulk sales, distance from the market is the critical factor. For high quality material distance is not a problem — the market for veneer quality oak, ash, and cherry was reported to be international, with buyers from France and Germany willing to take all that the market could supply.

5.12 There is also an element of fashion in types of timber. At the time of the survey oak was fashionable for furniture and joinery, with top quality planking commanding a price similar to imported mahogany and teak. This was not so about twenty years ago, and the situation may well be different again in another twenty years, but it is a factor which saw-millers and timber merchants have to live with.

5.13 There is a vivid contrast between the limited local use now made of small woods and the substantial exploitation which took place up to World War I and, to a considerable extent, until the end of World War II, with both wars having a significant effect on demands for forest produce. Edlin [17] and [18] and other writers such as Rose [64] and Sturt [67] show that until the recent past almost all woodland material, from coppice to the bark, branches, and twigs of standards, had some local use, and even the location of the tree and the compass direction of different sections of the trunk could be important ([65] p.36). One is reminded of the countryman's old claim to be able to use every part of a pig except its squeal. But these traditional markets have dwindled, and in some cases disappeared.

5.14 As with agriculture until World War II, the home-grown timber industry has had to (and still must) face competition from overseas without tariff protection, and so the price of home-grown timber has been largely determined by the low cost of exploiting virgin forests in other lands. The excellent manufacturing quality of this imported timber, with its long, straight lengths, has made obsolescent the old wood-working technology based on British hardwood coppice, pollards, and open-grown standards.

5.15 Also, the traditional markets have declined (or indeed collapsed) due to cultural and technological reasons. We no longer need wooden carts, metal wheelbarrows are handier and cheaper than those made of home-grown timbers, our whitewood kitchen tables have been replaced by plastic-topped units. These are examples of the reasons given for the lack of demand for species like sycamore, birch, poplar, alder and willow. We do not wholly accept this. It is arguable that new markets could have been developed. It was suggested that alder could not now be sold because people no longer wear clogs, but it finds a much wider use abroad [68]. There are local markets for alder for turnery but, given the generally straight, clean nature of much of the alder we saw, its further use as a timber could well be developed. Similar arguments could be put forward for other timbers, strengthened by the fact that they are (apart, perhaps, from willow) already commonly used in some areas. Lime is another species for which there is supposed to be no British demand, but we have heard reports of woodcarvers being unable to obtain supplies.

5.16 There was a small degree of interest, expressed by farm managers and landowners, in using timber from their woodlands on their own farms or estates. One owner in East Sussex sends his oak to a nearby saw-mill for conversion, paying a charge for the service. (Another approach exists in South Devon, where a contractor who takes his mobile saw-mill to a wood and converts logs on the spot for cash or half the produce has more business than he can handle.) From the evidence of the study areas and our background discussions, it is difficult to avoid the thought that some of the neglect of woodlands is due to entrepreneurial failure as well as to competition and dying markets.

5.17 A contributory factor, however, is the lack of continuity in supplies. (As one spokesman put it: "It is always either feast or famine".) After the feast of elm resulting from the present epidemic of elm disease ceases, many saw-mills may face a bleak future. Uncertainty of supply has been endemic, and more than one miller remarked that they were often unable to forecast their supplies beyond three months ahead. In Cornwall this situation has led, in a chicken and egg fashion, to a lack of capacity and a moribund local market.

5.18   The other major point of interest, that of a wood's total value of saleable timber resources, is linked to this problem of supply. The study has yielded clear evidence that, despite the adverse factors of small size, neglect, abuse, unwanted timber species and difficulties of access, many woodlands do have a significant value both to farmers and landowners on one hand and saw-millers and timber merchants on the other. These woodlands are a valuable resource which is not, at present, properly exploited to the benefit of either of the two parties or, as we argue in Chapter 2, to that of the nation.

5.19   It would of course make a nonsense of conservation objectives to clearfell these woods but, bearing in mind the arguments in the previous chapter for at least some positive management, together with the cost of such management and the reactions of farmers to such costs, it is right to consider whether there is a case for realising the value of some of this timber. It must be said at once, however, that by not clearfelling there is a reduction in the quantity of removable produce, which would considerably reduce the values shown in Table 3. Nevertheless, from the total value of about £838,000 it should be possible to achieve a periodic yield (over, say, each decade) of perhaps £100,000.

5.20   It is also worth noting that if the woods had been properly maintained in the past their absolute and sustained yield values would be considerably higher. A very rough measure of their potential annual value can be calculated by assuming a median yield class for one common hardwood species such as ash. A yield class of 8 indicates a potential growth of eight cubic metres a year which, at a typical price for second-quality planking, would, other things being equal, produce about £220 per hectare per year, or around £138,000 per year over the nine study areas. However, this is a hypothetical gross cash flow figure, against which would need to be set the costs of management. It also ignores the question of compound interest and assumes that timber production is the prime objective of woodland management, which clearly would not be the case over the whole nine study areas and their 461 woods.

5.21   A third important point, not apparent from the tables, is the question of imbalance between farms. On some farms, the woodlands are extremely valuable, whilst on others, the opposite is true. In the more valuable woods it is probable that sufficient cash flow could be generated by crown thinning and group felling to pay for management and other essential work, such as fencing and replanting needed to put the woods on a long-term productive base. But unfortunately this is not true of most of the woods surveyed. Rehabilitating many of the less valuable woods would leave the farmer or landowner with substantial costs to cover, even allowing for grants. A related aspect is that small woods are much more expensive to fence per unit area, bearing in mind that fencing is a major element of management costs (Table 5 (page 40) and paragraphs 5.38 and 5.39).

Game

5.22   Almost any woodland has some potential for game and, in this sense, the woods in the study areas therefore have potential for game management. The main factors are:

> i.   the local climate and topography of the area, with height and wind exposure being adverse factors for most game birds;

> ii.   the woods themselves, with dryness and warmth being valuable advantages for encouraging pheasant, similarly ponds and boggy patches for duck, and ground cover and a supply of berried shrubs being attractive to all birds;

> iii.   the relationship of the woods to each other in terms of distance apart, direction of major axes and edges;

> iv.   the relationship of the woods to other landscape features, such as hedges and banks, for gathering and flushing game;

> v.   the size and number of holdings and the tenure of the woods, there being minimum areas of land suitable for full shoot management;

> vi.   the agriculture of the area, with cereal growing usually being a beneficial factor, and a pool of local labour helpful for beating;

> vii.   the amount of access by the general public.

5.23   There is some informal shooting in all the areas studied, but organised keepered shoots were found only in Cambridgeshire, Lincolnshire and Warwickshire. Individual attempts at game management were found in Clwyd, East Sussex and North Yorkshire. ('Game' here includes the shooting of pheasant, partridge, wildfowl and deer, as well as the rough shooting of hare, rabbit, woodcock, pigeon etc. However, in the woods in the study areas (with the exception of Warwickshire), the main potential is for pheasant shooting.) The range of options for managing a pheasant shoot is fairly wide, from the simple encouragement of wild birds by feeding tail corn, through improvements to the woodland cover, to the full scale breeding, feeding and releasing of poults.

5.24   These options interlock with other factors. The sport may simply be for the owner's or shooting tenant's pleasure, or for the owner and his friends on a reciprocal basis. A more organised use may involve various syndicates; for example the owner plus friends on a cost-sharing basis, or the owner plus the sale of 'guns' or 'part guns', or the sale of shooting rights to an outside syndicate. At the really commercial end there are shooting holidays or shooting on a day-ticket basis.

5.25   These game pheasant options may be combined with wildfowl flight-shooting by encouraging wildfowl through improving ponds, judiciously removing high trees to improve flight paths, and providing feed corn. And wildfowl management, like rough shooting of woodcock, hare, and rabbit, may be pursued for its own sake. Deer-stalking is another activity for which the East Sussex and Warwickshire woods have some potential, but it would, in all probability, be difficult to realise. (The game consultant suggests that: "There are few game animals available to us in Britain over which more petty jealousy, professional misconduct, possessiveness, illegalities, and secrecy exist, than deer".) Unless combined with pheasant shooting, these other game activities are not usually syndicated but may be available on a holiday or day-ticket basis.

5.26   However, we have not found it possible to quantify game values, both present and potential, for three reasons:

    i.   respondents were unwilling to divulge financial data;

    ii.   most of the shooting is not 'sold off' but enjoyed as a hobby by owners or tenants;

    iii.   the potential value depends mainly on social, not physical factors.

5.27   In general, the game consultant felt that in Cambridgeshire, Lincolnshire and Warwickshire, where keepered areas are only a relatively small proportion of the total, there is room for further exploitation. In Clwyd, East Sussex and North Yorkshire, there is considerable physical potential which at present is not tapped to any great extent. In Cornwall, Gwent and Somerset, although the woods are suitable (given the correct management), there are a variety of problems related to climate, predators and inability to co-operate with neighbours which pose difficult problems. Co-operation is of critical importance in all areas, since an organised, managed shoot, offering six to eight good pheasant drives a day on several days in a season would ideally need to be 300 to 400 hectares in area—a size of holding not often found in the areas studied. It would also need perhaps eight farmers to make the cost of a keeper and the cost of release pens, feed, etc, reasonably bearable.

5.28   Woods were regarded as very necessary for successful game management in the study areas. But they are now at the stage where considerable management work is needed if their value for game is to be maintained, let alone improved. The reasons for this are similar to those noted previously: too much shade reducing the understorey and ground vegetation, thus making the woods draughty and reducing feed and shelter; spindly and 'leggy' trees at the edge of many woods; bareness and some disturbance caused by sheep and rabbit grazing.

5.29   Although new plantations will have some good game-holding characteristics after a few years, it is better, on balance, to maintain tree cover. The necessary felling could be carried out gradually in sections working over the woods slowly to control light and micro-climate and to avoid disturbing the game. Simply opening up the canopy is all that is needed in many cases. In others, group planting would help enrich the woods, as would underplanting and edge-planting with berry species and, along the woodland fringes, evergreen shrubs such as box and shrub honeysuckle. As noted above, cleaning out ponds and removing trees from flight paths would favour wild duck. Open areas and field edges near to woods could be sown with fodder crops which could also be cut for horses and cattle. Control of stock grazing and rabbits would be essential, together with predator control. Some additional planting on new ground to assist with holding and flushing birds would also be of benefit. Judicious widening of rides would be needed to break up larger woodlands into manageable blocks.

The Management Implications

5.30 In the previous chapter we set out some principles which could be mutually advantageous for the landscape and wildlife aspects of small woodlands (paragraph 4.50). The following paragraphs show that they are also sensible in relation to forestry, timber production and game conservation, and to wishes and needs of farmers.

5.31   It is apparent that the main objectives of woodland management for game conservation do not conflict to any marked extent with those for landscape and wildlife conservation: woodlands are important and sometimes critical for all three. The introduction of exotic trees and bushes for game shelter and feed may be contrary to one of Peterken's principles [61], but there is usually a native species suitable. In any case, such principles are directed at woods of high nature conservation importance and, as many of the more derelict smaller woods are not important in this respect, it should not be looked upon as a constraint.

5.32   The implications for timber and other forest produce, although less clear-cut, are perhaps best expressed in the clear facts that woods managed entirely for other purposes can also have a significant timber production value, and that the continuation of long-established woodland management (or some approximation of it) is necessary if most of the other values are to be maintained. If one takes the narrow view that forestry is for profitable timber production only, then there is clearly some sacrifice in, for instance, leaving mature trees standing for their wildlife and landscape value, or accepting the extra costs implied by the high intensity of management needed for irregular shelterwood or group systems. Most contentious of all perhaps is the loss incurred by not replacing existing tree stocks with faster-growing species and varieties. Against this economic sacrifice may be set the social and environmental benefits discussed in the previous chapter. The more acceptable view of the role of foresters is a wider one—the use of their woodland management skills for more socially determined ends (with the understanding that the social subsumes the economic). This was the view accepted by an older generation of foresters (see, for instance, Brasnett [4]), but it has been called into question in more recent years by a harder school of forest economists (such as Johnstone, Grayson, and Bradley [38]), Osmaston [55], and Gane [28] who, quite properly, seek to quantify or otherwise examine the non-timber benefits of forests, but who may have clouded the issue for some of their readers.

5.33   We argue in Chapter 2 that, for small woods (and because of the different outlooks of their owners), conventional forest economics are not always appropriate. This argument is underpinned in the following paragraphs which show how diverse the woodlands, their owners' objectives, and, therefore, the range of management options are. Simple costs and returns are given, together with discounted costs and returns where appropriate. A discount rate of 5 per cent has been used with constant prices (the estimated real rate of return on investments in the capital market [33]). The examples are based on real woods and real owners but are otherwise hypothetical. They set out to demonstrate that although it is difficult to generalise, and although a range of different approaches may be necessary (some demanding high capital and maintenance costs), a low key, low cost approach can be an entirely practical way to improve woods, both economically and physically.

5.34   **Example 1: Gwent.** A wood of 6.1 hectares, on a moderate slope down to a stream. Access is by means of a track along the top edge of the wood. The wood was formerly coppice with standards, largely clearfelled sixteen years prior to the survey, and has a few poor to reasonable oak standards over a rich mixture of coppice and self-sown trees, mainly birch (general yield class 12). The area is rich in plant life, but grazing—mainly by neighbours' sheep—is slowly reducing the undergrowth. The wood is not readily visible from the main roads. The owner values it mainly for its amenity but is not averse to taking a profit if it can be done without adverse effects on the wood. There is a good hardwood pulp market nearby, and the owner is also interested in the sale of cut logs for fuel. He is prepared to do the fencing himself (with family help). The best compromise between amenity, wildlife conservation and profitability (taking into account the previous management history) would be to manage it on a pulpwood rotation. Dividing it into two roughly equal areas, each would be cut over at fourteen years old, and the bulk of the crop sold for pulpwood. Unsuitable produce could be corded at rideside and cut for firewood for domestic use and for sale. Sale would be standing to contractors, with the stipulation that a scatter of trees should be left for seed, otherwise no silvicultural treatment would be needed. Fencing would be necessary to keep out livestock but need not be rabbit-proof. For the first coupe the expenditure and income would be something like this:

Expenditure	£
Fencing	
(Half of area: materials only) 750 metres @ £1	750
Maintenance of fences, ditches, and track	100
	850

Income

Sale of 3 ha. pulpwood (210 tonnes @ £1 standing)	210
Small woods grant @ £250 per ha[1]	750
	960

Balance of income over expenditure	£110

[1]Payable when area is successfully regenerated—at, say, three years, discounted at 5% the present value would be £648.

The owner is interested in the possibility of harvesting and delivering the pulpwood as a family enterprise. This would increase the return from the sale of pulpwood by adding value—the gross return would be approximately £2,000—but there would be the additional costs of plant, machinery and transport. There might also be a debit item for the opportunity cost of his and his family's employment on other farm enterprises. In real terms, costs would be similar in seven years' time when the next coupe would be due, but the yield of pulpwood would be higher.

5.35 **Example 2: East Sussex.** A ten-hectare wood of oak, ash and sycamore over chestnut coppice, fenced and ditched, with arable fields around. The soil is sandy and the wood is well drained, with a network of rides throughout and access via all-weather farm roads. The standards are semi-mature and some crown thinning is needed. The coppice is heavily overgrown, threatening the quite varied ground vegetation. No grazing is allowed. The wood is on a wholly managed estate with a farm labour force of eight men, two of whom are also skilled coppice craftsmen. The owners wish to retain the broadleaved character of the wood for its amenity, but would like it to contribute something to the farm income. Labour can easily be spared in winter, but not capital. It is recommended that the whole wood should be crown thinned over a period of five years and the sawn timber obtained used for estate purposes. Small-scale group planting of replacement oak is advised for the broader gaps to augment natural regeneration. The chestnut coppice should be partly cut for a stockpile of posts and split stakes and rails, and the remaining coppice should be divided into five equal coupes and sold standing for charcoal at two-year intervals. The simple costs and returns are shown below, but note that this plan of operations would not be eligible for Forestry Commission grants.

Expenditure (ten-year period)	*Actual* £	*Present Value*[1] £
Maintenance of fences and ditches	250	193 (10)
750 Oak whips 1–1.2 metres, Netlon guards, staples, ties	1,000	772 (10)
Labour: planting and weeding, 40 man/days	500	386 (10)
cutting and hauling produce, 100 man/days	1,250	1,082 (5)
Machinery: fuel and depreciation, 200 hours @ £3	600	520 (5)
Ripping charge (saw-mill) 100 cubic metres @ £17	1,700	1,472 (5)
	5,300	4,425

Income (ten year period)		
Value of fenceposts/stakes/rails (sufficient for 2 km fence @ £500 per km)	1,000	866 (5)
Value of sawn timber, 60 cubic metres @ £150	9,000	7,793 (5)
Value of fuel for two houses[2]	2,600	2,008 (10)
Sale of standing coppice (plus lop and top) for charcoal, 10 ha @ £200	2,000	1,544 (10)
	14,600	12,211

Balance of Income over Expenditure	9,300	7,786

[1]Present value of a series of costs and returns (over the period of years shown in brackets) discounted at 5%
[2]Assumes equivalent of two tons of coal per year for two houses @ £60 per ton.

(It is arguable that, on the one hand, farm overheads (including management) should be charged on woodland operations; and on the other that, since both farm management and farm labour costs are fixed, the real cost of both to this marginal operation would be zero.)

5.36   Example 3: Cambridgeshire. A six hectare wood purchased by the owner for shooting and amenity. The owner manages it as a hobby, using his garden for a nursery (mainly oak from acorns collected in the wood). The wood is very open from past felling and neglect and, partly because of its variation in physical structure, is very rich in plant and other wildlife. Management, which is for shooting, amenity, and wildlife, is a lively family affair with working picnics and weekend visits. Rides are kept fairly open for shooting. Elsewhere oak trees are planted and maintained in ones and twos, and natural regeneration is encouraged. The owner has an interest in woodland management (including antiquarian books on the subject). The general policy is one of slow enrichment. No return is looked for, but the owner hopes that it will be of economic benefit to a future generation. No alternative prescription is needed.

Expenditure and Income: impossible to quantify.

5.37   Example 4: Lincolnshire. A wood of 1.4 hectares which was formerly a plantation of ash and oak (on old rigg and furrow). It has been neglected for many years, with the result that the stems are relatively slender and are putting on very little diameter growth. There is a scattering of other species, including wild cherry, willow and hawthorn but its wildlife value is low relative to other nearby woods. The wood is fenced and is surrounded by arable fields, so grazing is not a problem. There is a ride through the wood and an all-weather road is some 100 metres away. The owner uses the wood only for game cover, but is aware that some further management is needed. He is keenly interested in and appreciative of his woodlands, and is clearing an older wood nearby by removing suppressed stems and windblown trees. However, his time is very limited. Fairly heavy crown thinning is recommended to remove perhaps a third of the standing trees. Very few of the felled trees would be of merchantable size, and there would be no return from this operation. It is suggested that the felled trees be trimmed and stacked at rideside for firewood—either domestic or for sale as a small timber or firewood lot. The costs and returns would be roughly as follows:

	£
Expenditure	
Labour[1] 30 man/days @ £13	390
Machinery: fuel and depreciation, 150 hours @ £3	450
Maintenance and repair of fences	50
	890
Income	
Oak etc, fenceposts[2]	50
Fuel to farmhouse[3]	926
	976
Balance of Income over Expenditure	86

[1]Standard agricultural rate for skilled worker
[2]A nominal fee
[3]The present value of an estimated flow of benefits over a ten-year Period at 5% compound interest. The annuity is based on the cost of two tons of coal equivalent per year @ £60 per ton.

5.38   Example 5: Somerset. This is a former wood, felled and burned over, on an exposed sloping area of two hectares. It carries a few birch trees but the cover is mainly bracken and gorse. It is unfenced and the surrounding fields are used for stock. There are rabbits in the area. The owner is keenly interested in the landscape value of woods and would like to do something to improve this rather ugly slope, but has little time or money to spare. The only practicable approach is to replant the area completely. The owner would wish to see at least some broadleaved trees planted, but would also like to see some produce useful for the farm. The suggestion is to establish oak and sweet chestnut, with a Japanese Larch nurse crop (the larch for small sawlogs, the chestnut for coppicing for fenceposts, etc, and the oak to grow on as standards), the whole operation to be carried out by a contractor. The costs and returns would be approximately as follows:

Expenditure			£	£
Labour:	preparation of ground (cutting out gorse)			
	10 man/days @ £13		130	
	rabbit eradication, 10 man/days @ £13		130	
	planting, 5 man/days @ £13		65	
	weeding (at 4 years), 20 man/days @ £13		260	
			—	
				585
Fencing:	stock- and rabbit-proof, 800 m @ £2.50			2,000
	(including erection costs)			
Plants:	Initial planting, 2.5 m × 2.0 m			
	1,200 oak 1 + 1 @ £120 per 1,000		144	
	1,000 sweet chestnut 1 + 1 @ £130 per 1,000		130	
	1,000 Japanese larch 1 + 1 @ £50 per 1,000		50	
			—	
				324
	Beating up, 500 plants mixed spp.			50
				2,959
Income				
	Forestry Commission grants			600
Balance of Expenditure over Income				2,359

In fact, at these costs the owner could not afford to carry out the work. The major costs are in the fencing and labour and so a switch to, say, pure conifers or more use of herbicides etc, would not significantly affect the figures.

5.39 The impact of the cost of new fencing is so high that it is a critical factor in the management of small woods, and it is worth going to considerable lengths to avoid such expenditure. Table 5 shows the theoretical average cost of fencing woods of different sizes and seriously calls into question the present practice of a flat rate of grant aid per hectare.

Table 5 Grant-aid Obtainable for Planting or Re-planting Small Broadleaved Woods in Comparison with Fencing Costs

Size of wood (hectares)	(acres)	Perimeter if square (m)	Appropriate grant	Amount of grant	Fencing costs[1] (£)	Balance Actual (£)	per hectare (£)
0.1	0.25	124	Countryside Commission	40–60%	217	(−109)	(−1,090)
0.2	0.49	176	,, ,,	40–60%	308	(−154)	(−770)
0.25	0.62	200	Forestry Commission Small Woods	£75	350	−275	−1,100
0.5	1.24	284	,, ,,	£150	497	−347	−536
0.75	1.85	348	,, ,,	£225	609	−384	−512
1.0	2.47	400	,, ,,	£300	700	−400	−400
1.5	3.71	488	,, ,,	£450	854	−404	−269
2.0	4.94	564	,, ,,	£600	987	−387	−194
2.5	6.18	632	,, ,,	£750	1,106	−356	−142
3.0	7.41	692	,, ,,	£750	1,211	−461	−154
4.0	9.88	800	,, ,,	£1,000	1,400	−400	−100
5.0	12.35	896	,, ,,	£1,250	1,568	−318	−64
6.0	14.82	980	,, ,,	£1,500	1,715	−215	−36
7.0	17.29	1,060	,, ,,	£1,750	1,855	−105	−15
8.0	19.76	1,132	,, ,,	£2,000	1,981	+19	+2

Table 5   Grant-aid Obtainable for Planting or Re-planting Small Broadleaved Woods in Comparison with Fencing Costs—contd.

Size of wood (hectares)	(acres)	Perimeter if square (m)	Appropriate grant		Amount of grant	Fencing costs[1] (£)	Balance Actual (£)	per hectare (£)
9.0	22.23	1,200	,,	,,	£2,250	2,100	+150	+17
9.5	23.47	1,232	,,	,,	£2,375	2,156	+219	+23
10.0	24.70	1,264	Forestry Commission Basis III		£2,250	2,212	+38	+4
11.0	27.17	1,324	,,	,,	£2,475	2,317	+158	+14

[1]Fencing costs are estimated assuming the wood to need fencing all round, fencing cost £1.75 per metre, and the wood to be square. Other shaped woods might need slightly shorter but would probably need considerably longer fences. Irregular shapes would incur higher labour costs.

A Note on Taxation

5.40   It is not within the remit of this study to present a detailed exposition of the effects of taxation on small woodlands, but it would be naïve to disregard it altogether. The subject has been well covered by Hart [32], and it is understood from this that the owner must be assessed for Income Tax in respect of woods managed on a commercial basis *and* with a view to the realisation of profits. This assessment would be under either Schedule B or Schedule D. For most of the examples quoted above, assessment under Schedule B would mean a very small tax to pay (commonly 33 pence per hectare per year). For Example 5, the heavy investment necessary might indicate a shift to Schedule D, which enables the owner to set off the costs involved against other taxable income. With care and forethought, woodland owners can avoid serious taxation of woodland income. If woods are managed solely for their amenity, then they are not liable to tax. There is no Capital Gains Tax on the trees, only on the land, but Capital Transfer Tax is payable. In general, the taxation system recognises the great benefit of woodlands to the nation, and that forestry is a long-term investment with rather low returns.

Figure 5
Sizes of Respondents' Farms Summary
Shown by percentage

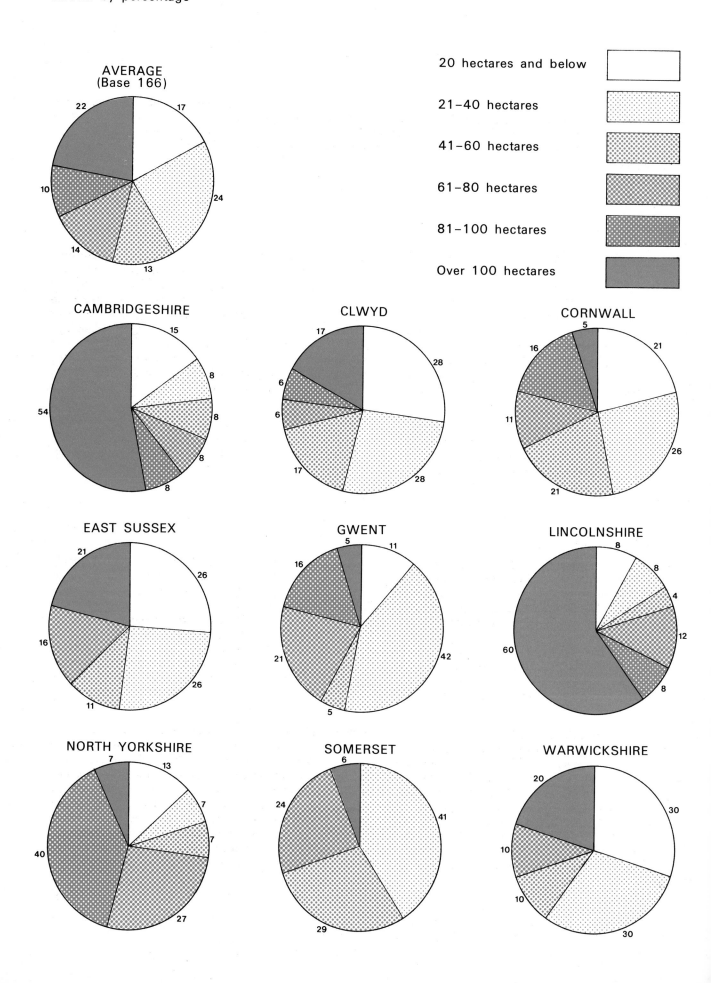

6 The Farmer's Attitudes

6.1 We held interviews (from half-an-hour to two hours) with 165 farmers, landowners, managers, agents and others involved in making decisions on woodland management, and more fleeting contact was made with at least another 100 farmers, landowners and agents. In all they represent a very wide social and economic spectrum, ranging from the tenants of a Cornish smallholding to the owner-occupier of a 400-hectare arable farm in East Anglia.

General

6.2 The attitudes of farmers and landowners to the survey teams and to the survey itself are interesting. Owing largely to the help received from the National Farmers' Union, the Farmers' Union of Wales, the Country Landowners' Association and the Royal Institution of Chartered Surveyors, little innate hostility was met with, but there was a considerable amount of scepticism and suspicion. The suspicions arose partly from the general level of irritation felt by farmers towards interruptions to their busy lives from the significant number of people who call at farms for commercial reasons. It also arose from a wide dislike of government 'snooping', and it was necessary several times to explain that the survey was nothing to do with the Inland Revenue Department, the Forestry Commission, or the local authority and that the confidentiality of the material being collected would be respected. (This suspicion has implications for the policy-related conclusions in Chapters 2 and 3).

6.3 The following appraisal is borne out in the main by evidence from other relevant surveys, such as those carried out by the Ministry of Agriculture, Fisheries and Food's Agricultural Development and Advisory Service [2]; by Worthington [75] and Newby and his colleagues [54] and from our own limited previous work [9]. However, it is based entirely on the interviews carried out in the course of the survey, unless otherwise stated.

Landscape

6.4 Our judgments on farmers' attitudes, which are summarised in Figures 6, 7 and 8, were made subjectively after the interviews. Thus farmers answering our carefully composed, neutral questions on uses made of their woods were scaled higher if mention was made, for example, of the varied greens of the oaks in spring; and higher still if amenity trees had been planted. In Figure 6 the judgments on attitudes to 'woods and trees in general' and 'woods in the landscape' are taken together, as being different facets of the same set of attitudes. They are expressed in percentages for greater ease of interpretation, but the bases are approximately as shown in Figure 5 (in Gwent, two respondents were too reticent for their attitudes to be assessed at all; and in Cornwall, no attitude towards 'landscape' was discernable from one respondent). Over two-thirds of the people interviewed spontaneously expressed more than a mild interest in trees, woods, and landscape conservation; and less than a fifth were totally indifferent or antagonistic.

6.5 Despite these stated or revealed attitudes a comparison of what farmers and landowners said they did (or did not do) with their woods and the reality on the ground gives some cause for concern, and we became aware of a considerable ambivalence in the minds of many farmers. There is first the considerable public concern about changes to the environment resulting from the intensification of farming activity in the last three decades, and there can be few farmers and landowners who are not aware of the debate on conservation and agriculture. Consequently many may express a general sympathy towards the landscape (especially to strangers) without necessarily feeling any need to take personal action—rather like being 'against sin', when an expression of sympathy avoids arguments but commits one to nothing. On the other hand some farmers have undoubtedly felt impelled to strike a hard attitude towards what they see as woolly-headed nostalgia, perhaps less out of conviction than irritation. We suspect that these reactions underly a number of the interviews.

Figure 6
Attitudes to Woods and Landscape Summary
Shown by percentage

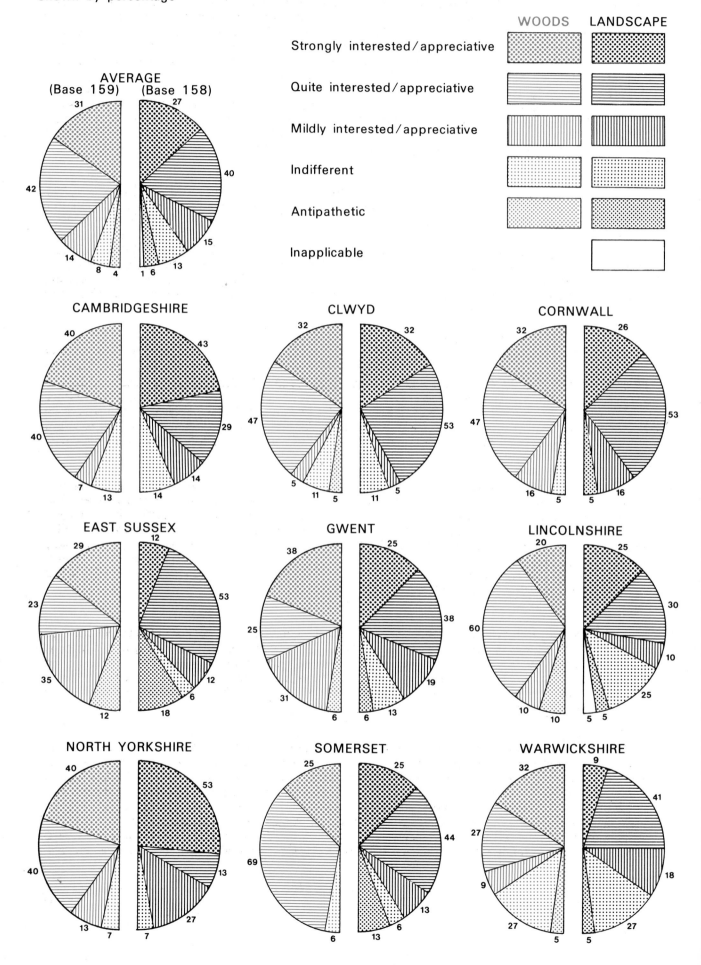

6.6   There are other undercurrents. In general we agree with Newby, Bell, Saunders and Rose [54], who have classified farmers and landowners into four categories: 'gentlemen farmers', 'family farmers', 'active managerial farmers', and 'agri-businessmen', and also with Worthington [75], who has shown that land agents also have an important influence on the practices adopted on institutionally owned farms. But the attitudes of these groupings to their woods are by no means direct relationships. We feel that the differences in attitude—and between attitude and behaviour—arise from farmers' and landowners' own perceptions of small woods, and from their differences in awareness to them. For example, it is likely that many of those who were born and spent their childhood on a farm, and who have a lifetime's contact with the countryside and a knowledge of its wildlife and environment, feel an empathy and an intuitive response to their environment (read for example Page [57]). Indeed, many older countrymen who derive at least part of their livelihood from wildlife have a detailed knowledge of its habitats [72]. However, this almost subliminal knowledge and appreciation has only recently begun to link in farmers' and landowners' minds with their day-to-day agricultural practice. We suggest that this linking of cause and effect is by no means widespread, especially for woodlands.

6.7   Thus most of the farmers and landowners we talked to have a fair appreciation of woods and trees as visible aspects of their farm and its surroundings but do not perceive them as entities in their own right. Their use is entirely agricultural (for grazing, shelter and the odd fencepost), domestic (for fuel), recreation (to walk or ride in, or for game) or just to look at. A fair number are conscious of their potential for agriculture or forestry, and it is this group who are the most active in clearing and replanting. But there is very little awareness of woods either as wildlife habitats or—and this is the crux—as the timber production enterprise which many once were. This is probably due primarily to lack of knowledge, and from talks both with farmers and the timber trade may arise first from the working of the traditional landlord-tenant system, and secondly from the way in which most of the smaller woods were once 'managed'.

6.8   During the period 1887–91 (not long ago in the life of a tree), 82 per cent of occupiers were tenants (of about 85 per cent of the total area of crops and grass), compared to 47 per cent in 1960 (of about 49 per cent of the total agricultural area) [47]. By 1977, 54 per cent of all agricultural land in England and 67 per cent in Wales was owner-occupied [48]. It was normal estate practice to retain the woods in hand, and most farmers had nothing to do with managing them. Consequently there was no experience of woodland management to pass on to succeeding, often younger, farmers. There was also sometimes a significant degree of hostility felt by tenants to woods on their farms (still apparent to a degree in Wales, where the owner was usually English or Anglo-Welsh).

6.9   The second possible cause is a linked one. For most of their history, the now 'ancient' woodlands were 'managed' in a form of continuous husbandry, usually, and until quite recently, by the user of the timber. Thus saw-millers, carpenters, wheelwrights, cartwrights and coppice craftsmen such as hurdlemakers, bodgers, clog-sole cutters and a host of others [18] would make an offer for, purchase, fell, haul and process standing timber, coppice and even whole woods. They were in many cases, the stewards of the woods, with a strong degree of enlightened self-interest in sustaining the yield over a wide area. Rackham distinguishes this form of management from forestry, calling it 'woodmanship' [63] but its influence waned as the traditional markets declined from the late nineteenth century onwards.

6.10   But the legacy of this tradition is, again, a lack of knowledge and expertise in woods and their management by most farmers and a great many landowners. More important, the decline of the traditional markets and associated activities has broken the links between farmers and potential markets, and this is a significant factor in the deterioration of small woodlands. Farmers know little of forestry and little of timber and, perhaps, have no one that they can trust to advise them or take on the commercial transactions so that their woods could produce a useful income.

6.11   The misconceptions held by farmers and landowners of the value of their woods help to explain their ambivalent attitudes towards them. If they have no other apparent function and do not appear to be damaged, why not at least use them for sheltering stock? Why should farmers be concerned about woodlands when they have never done more than occasionally respond to an approach from a coppice craftsman (who has now probably retired)? If woods have no function, bring in no income, and are havens for weeds or pests, why not reclaim them? One does not need to cite the profit motive (which is inherent in the conservation versus intensive agriculture debate) to explain the slow erosion of woodland cover from the countryside. The financial aspects are discussed in paragraphs 6.15 to 6.19: but it is helpful first to look at attitudes to wildlife and game conservation.

Figure 7
Attitudes to Wildlife and Game Summary

Shown by percentage

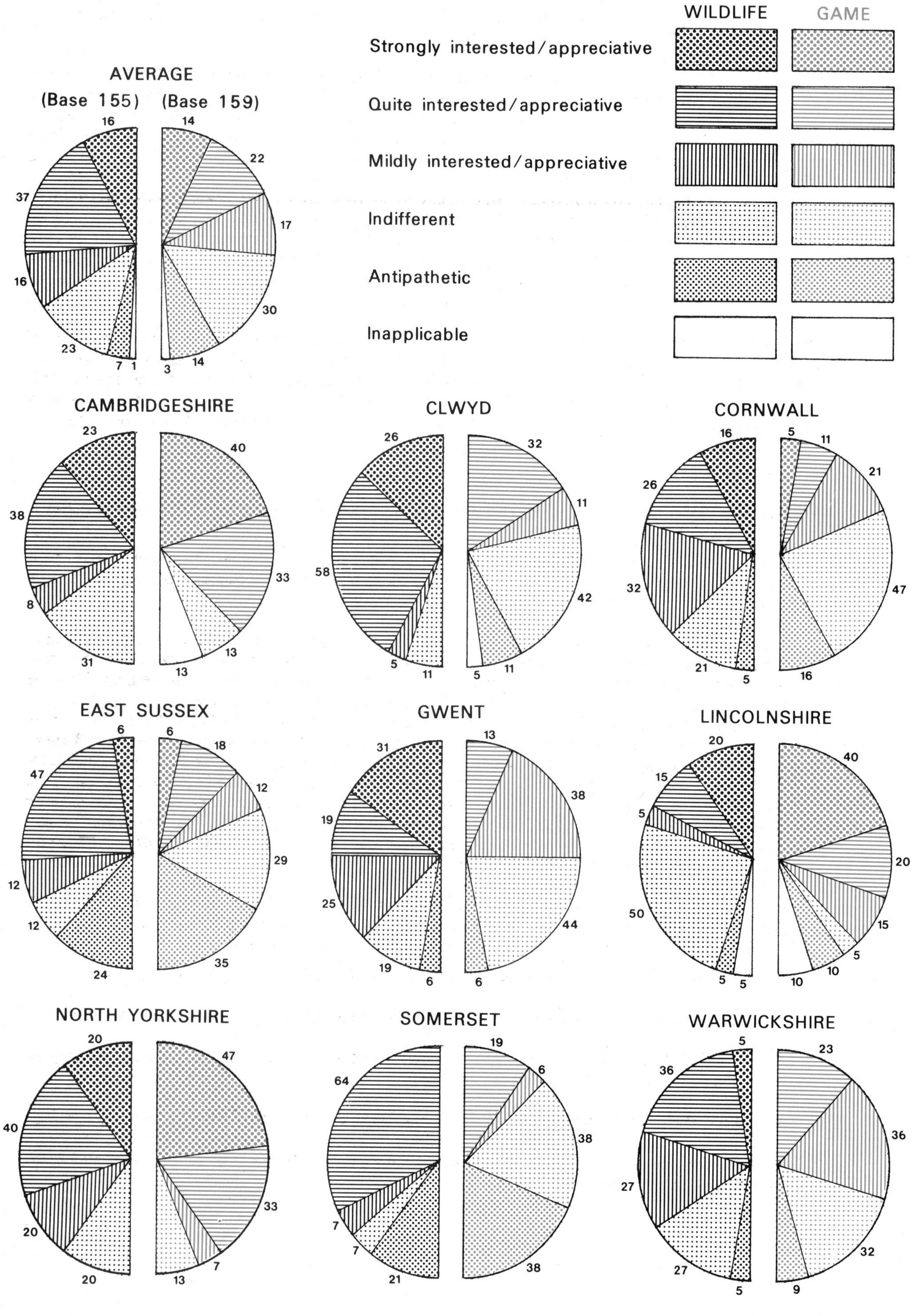

WILDLIFE   GAME

Strongly interested/appreciative

Quite interested/appreciative

Mildly interested/appreciative

Indifferent

Antipathetic

Inapplicable

Wildlife and Game

6.12 Farmers' and landowners' attitudes to wildlife and game (Figure 7) were less easily revealed in conversation than their attitudes to woods and the landscape. Also attitudes to wildlife and attitudes to game differ — not only from study area to area, but also within individual areas—to a much greater extent than attitudes to woods in the landscape.

6.13 Attitudes to game aspects of woodlands are far from straightforward. There is certainly keen interest in the potential for shooting in the counties of Cambridgeshire, Lincolnshire and North Yorkshire; but much less in the two other 'shooting counties' of East Sussex and Warwickshire. There is some pattern to the consistently low interest in the western counties which relates to the influence of climate, topography and size of holdings. As noted earlier (paragraph 5.22 *et seq*) size of holding is critical, and it is well understood that, co-operative efforts excepted, any investment in game management would be to the benefit of one's neighbours. So nothing is done. One or two farmers have tried attracting wild pheasant but have given it up. There is some indication of willingness to co-operate to improve mutual enjoyment, but there is also evidence of the break-up of previous syndicates (partly to avoid quarrelling with a neighbour in one case, and to avoid asking a member to leave in another). Despite the physical circumstances being suitable (paragraph 5.27), because of these 'social' problems, the actual potential in most areas for improving the sporting interest of woods is small, particularly when the 14 per cent of farmers who are hostile to shooting is taken into account.

6.14 Attitudes to wildlife values of small woods are also very variable: taking together the two scales of 'strongly' and 'quite' appreciative, they vary from as high as 84 per cent with favourable attitudes in Clwyd down to 35 per cent in Lincolnshire. To a degree, this interest is in inverse relationship to the value placed on game (but Cambridgeshire scores high and Warwickshire low on both sets of values). Overall, nearly a third of the farmers are apparently indifferent or hostile towards the wildlife of their woods—a proportion which surprises us.

Financial Aspects

6.15 In the tables accompanying the case studies we classify farmers and landowners by the degree to which they expressed interest and anxiety regarding the financial aspects of woodland management. Figure 8 brings together the data from the case studies.

6.16 Taking the first two categories for each area and comparing them with the last two, there is a quite interesting pattern. Apart, perhaps, from Warwickshire and Somerset, the more prosperous farming areas appear to have the least interest in the money aspects of woodlands, and the least prosperous the most. To some extent, the interest in the least prosperous areas might be expected, but the lack of interest in the money side in the intensively farmed areas may be surprising to many. We believe the reason is probably that many of those who are now enjoying some prosperity are feeling able to move beyond the narrower role of profit-seeking to one of stewardship; it was expressed in almost those words by two Cambridgeshire farmers. Others expressed it as being a feeling that, now their agricultural enterprises were on a sound footing and the management of the farm was largely self-directing, they were able—indeed, overdue—to do something positive about their neglected woods (tidy them up). It is a little ironic to note that the prosperity promoted by intensive farming methods which has caused concern amongst conservationists may now lead, in some circumstances, to an upsurge of positive conservation measures.

6.17 The issues however are less clear than this pattern would indicate. Looking at the interviews (particularly the second interviews, after farmers had had time to reconsider) it seems to us that those with an interest in or concern for the money aspects of their woodlands can be divided into five groups:

    i.   those whose financial position is far from secure and who are looking for extra income;

    ii.   those who want their woods to be productive in a businesslike way ie for them to 'pay their way';

    iii.   those who are willing to make some improvements (or let someone else do it) providing they do not suffer financially;

    iv.   those who regard the high costs involved (and lack of return) as their reason for doing nothing;

    v.   those who look for some government contribution towards existing costs; for example, on fences or towards improving game conservation.

Figure 8
Attitudes towards Financial Aspects Summary
Shown by percentage

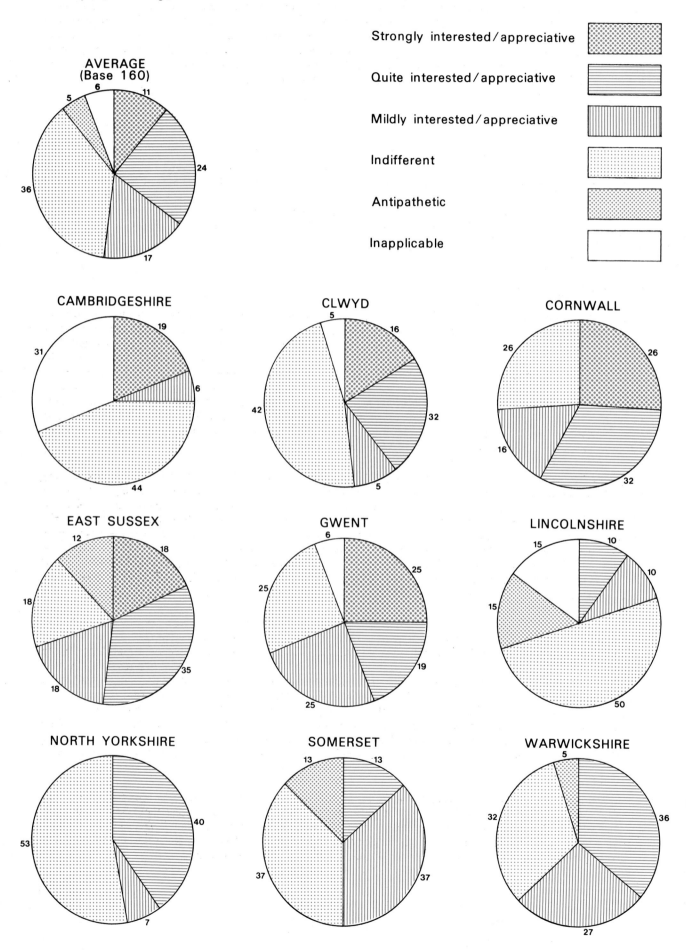

6.18   Consequently, there are those for whom money is either a goal or a constraint, and those for whom it is both. Where money was a constraint, there is keen interest in the grant-aid available. Where it is a goal, the interest is directed more towards increasing their knowledge. The reactions displayed following the tentative valuations of their potential woodland assets reflect these divisions. Woods worth, standing, about £800 were "peanuts" to one business-like and prosperous farmer; another with woods worth around £17,000 wanted to know to what degree he could safely exploit them to make them contribute towards the cost of a new stock bull. There was one landowner who wanted reassurance that the value of his woodland would cover the cost of clearing it for conversion to agriculture; and another (clearly needing time to recover from the shock of hearing that he was living amongst £50,000 worth of trees) asked about his tax position.

Taxation

6.19   A few farmers, particularly in Cornwall and Somerset, expressed some concern about the possible penal effect of Capital Transfer Tax on improved woodland. In general, however, tax (of any kind) does not appear to be a factor influencing either the present use made of woods on farms, or the attitudes of those interviewed towards managing them in the future. We did not deliberately raise the subject, so it is not possible to quantify this aspect in any way. However, our impression is that most of the farmers and landowners interviewed do not yet understand this new tax, and of those who do, most discount it in comparison to its effects on the remainder of their farm or estate.

Other Findings

6.20   Yet another aspect of farmers' and landowners' perception of woods is that they cannot have a positive, policy-related attitude to them without a basic knowledge of conservation, and a good proportion of the second interview was devoted to answering respondents' questions on how they should be managed. The demand for information often took over an hour to satisfy, and the questions were usually of two kinds: the strategic and the technical. A considerable proportion of the farmers interviewed for the second time wanted help in deciding what their management objectives should be. Only then was it possible to advise how they might be achieved. Normally, reference was made to other advisory sources: Forestry Commission, County Council, Countryside Commission, Nature Conservancy Council, County Trust for Nature Conservation, and the Farming and Wildlife Advisory Group. In the case of improvements to sporting interests, they were referred either to DART's own consultant or to the Game Conservancy.

6.21   Technical knowledge was sought mainly by those who already had a reasonably clear idea of what they wanted, or who needed to be reassured that the desired results were technically possible (avoiding weeding, for example). Some of the questions, such as the work study aspects of cutting firewood, or the physical problems of planting in groups, were quite difficult even for an experienced forester to answer. It became apparent that the farmer can contribute in a number of practical ways—for instance in using fertilisers or mulching plants with surplus straw to help keep the soil moist and reduce weeding. In fact, it is quite possible to speculate on a 'farm forestry' which is significantly different from normal commercial practice but which fits, in its methods and timing of operations, with the season-to-season management of the farm, and which brings in the farmer, where possible, to contribute a sizeable share of both skill and machinery.

6.22   In most study areas we met farmers and landowners who had experienced or knew of other farmers who had had unsatisfactory service from timber contractors. This had led to a deep suspicion of contractors and saw-millers. Its roots lie in the widely held opinion that owners have been cheated on the price paid for standing timber; in broken agreements which have left the poorer stems while 'creaming off' the good ones; in prices paid which have not covered the damage to farm roads, gates and fields caused by extracting the timber; and in the woods which have been left in a tangle of branchwood and knocked-down undergrowth. Some of the damage and waste was seen at first hand: for example, the woods in Gwent and North Yorkshire where the contractor had promised to return and remove the remaining (suppressed) larch, but had not done so; or where in cutting poles for turnery a contractor had felled good, straight cherry, removed only the top pole and left the valuable butts to rot. As a result two of the farmers interviewed had sworn never to allow a contractor into their woods again.

6.23   On the other hand we did meet a number of saw-millers who are proud of the reputation for honest dealing and careful work which they have built up with farmers and landowners; one which permits them to go back and negotiate further deals in subsequent years. Nevertheless even they admitted that fly-by-night contractors do exist, that saw-millers caught in the frequent down-swings of the trade have been known to cut corners, and that this sort of thing is very damaging to the home-grown timber trade as a whole.

Conclusions

6.24   The great majority of farmers in the study areas have an undeveloped but nevertheless genuine appreciation of their own woods and of woods in the landscape generally. A slightly smaller number are sympathetic towards wildlife in their woods, but with the proviso that it should not impinge adversely on their agricultural or sporting interests. A significant minority go beyond just sympathy to some degree of enthusiasm for different aspects of woods, notably their beauty, their wildlife, and their value for recreation (including, of course, shooting). On the other hand, a substantial minority—perhaps as high as one in five—are either indifferent or even hostile to woods and trees, for personal or financial reasons.

6.25   Despite the appreciation and sympathy, there is nevertheless a widespread lack of care for woods and, in many cases, positive abuse of them. Certainly it is not generally realised that woods need care. We feel this is due to a basically faulty perception of woodlands as an entity. Using the terms of the psychology of communication, woods are outside farmers 'schemata' or mental maps, and this can only be changed by a process of conscious thought about them together with new information. The 'schemata' are then modified by incorporating the new perception thus achieved—a process known as accommodation (see, for instance, Neisser [53] and Gibson [29]). In plain terms, the plight of woods must first be brought to the attention of farmers and landowners: then they must be offered adequate information to help them to reassess their attitudes and policies. It is probable that, simply by asking questions about their woods, and so drawing attention to them, a high degree of awareness of the problems can be created in the minds of many of those concerned. Even the deliberately low-key and neutral questions we asked in this survey perceptibly altered the attitudes of those interviewed in one direction or another.

6.26   We conclude from the interviews that goodwill does exist to alter the more unsatisfactory aspects of the condition of many woodlands, and that a significant minority of competent and well respected farmers and landowners will take action to improve their woods. They need help and advice to clarify their aims and objectives and to ensure that they do the right thing for the right reasons. With the other, larger, group if changes of attitude and positive action are to be encouraged, it will be necessary to go directly to them, to make them aware of their woods, give an honest appraisal of the prevailing conditions, and then offer the necessary advice and help. Most farmers and landowners in this group are usually too preoccupied with their day-to-day farming and other business to respond to less direct methods such as general publicity.

6.27   So far as promoting positive management action is concerned, there are constraints of time, money, detailed professional and technical information, and distrust of the forest produce market to overcome. For some, an awakened interest will mean a personal involvement in managing their woodlands (Example 1, paragraph 5.34); for others, management would have to be 'bought in' (Example 5, paragraph 5.38). In some cases, the value of the woodland crop will be such as to generate the cash flow necessary to manage the woods (Example 2, paragraph 5.35), or justify any expense arising from enjoyment of the improved shooting (Example 3, paragraph 5.36). In other cases, grant would help to tip the balance slightly (Example 4, paragraph 5.37). However, in many, and probably most woods, there will be a significant net cost to the farmer which cannot be easily justified, or even afforded. Clearly, as these greatly differing circumstances demonstrate, any national policies and financial aid towards woodland improvement will need to be very flexible.

Small woods...

. . . give character to the landscape
(a hidden valley in Cornwall)

. . . are essential habitats for a wide range
of wildlife
(old woodland in Warwickshire)

. . .can provide useful supplies of timber
(sweet chestnut in Somerset)

. . . are valuable for amenity and recreation
(a woodland walk in North Yorkshire)

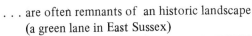

. . . are often remnants of an historic landscape
(a green lane in East Sussex)

A sample of the problems found in small woods during the course of the study...

Overgrown, unmanaged thickets and scrub

△◁
▽ Three examples of dereliction caused by grazing stock in unfenced woods

Damage caused (and left) by
contractors extracting timber

Conversion of old broadleaved woods
to coniferous plantations

Dumping of farm and other rubbish

The ravages of Dutch elm disease

The untapped resource of many small woods

Good hardwood timber in...

Gwent

East Sussex

Warwickshire

Lincolnshire

Cambridgeshire

Appendix I

Survey Methodology

First Interviews

1. Having broadly defined the scope of the study, the farmers were then identified and contacted on a sequential basis. The first contacts were made with the assistance of the local representative of the National Farmers' Union or the Farmers' Union of Wales, and wherever possible appointments to interview were arranged by telephone. During the interview, a deliberately neutral attitude was maintained. The interviews were structured (ie the surveyors had a checklist of information to be sought), but a good deal of information (especially about attitudes) was implicit in respondents' replies to simple questions about the location and history of their woods. Permission was sought to visit the woods to carry out the survey (not granted only in some areas where the woods were used for rearing pheasants, and for which a second visit was made after the shooting season). The boundaries of the holding or holdings were ascertained, together with information on neighbours, who were then, in turn, approached. Refusals to grant interviews or to provide data were recorded.

2. Farm boundaries were traced on to 6-inch Ordnance Survey maps and on to aerial photographs, where these could be obtained. In this way as complete a picture as possible was built up of the often complex ownership pattern in each area. Completion of the survey was not always possible within the three-week period allocated to each area—sometimes owners were abroad, ownership disputed, the numbers of farmers involved too many (Clwyd), or the land was managed by agents who needed to seek the owner's permission.

3. Apart from boundaries and ownership, specific information was sought on:

Holding

Size
Length of ownership or tenure
Stock
Crops
Other enterprises

Woodland

Cover
Origins
Management
Present uses
Past uses
Constraints
Grants or advice received

Attitudes to woods

General
Sporting
Wildlife
Landscape

Woodland Survey

4. **First Stage.** The first stage of the survey was a general assessment of each wood in each study area: depending on the size of wood this might take the team of two surveyors between one hour and one day. The surveyors were mostly graduates in a land management or biological discipline. After initial briefing and training at Dartington further training was carried out in the field—mainly in the Cornwall study area. Thereafter each team was given its own study area. To check the consistency of the data collected the teams were brought back together half-way through the survey period.

5. Managed woodlands were noted and assessed visually, but, as they were already being managed, thus indicating an existing interest by the owner, they were regarded as being outside the terms of reference of the study and were not surveyed in detail from the timber and wildlife aspects. No precise definition of exactly what constituted a managed woodland was available, and the final decision rested with DART's forester on the second round of visits. Broadly speaking, woods which, on verbal and physical evidence, were being managed to a fixed plan of operations were excluded. Woods which, according to available evidence, were subject to sporadic or *ad hoc* felling, clearing or planting were included. Woods which had been replanted under the *old* Small Woods Grant Scheme, but neglected thereafter, were included as *de facto* unmanaged.

6. **Second Stage.** After the data had been checked and processed at Dartington, second visits were made for the more specialised assessments of timber, landscape and game conservation. The timber appraisals were carried out by DART's forester, who visited each wood. Landscape and game appraisals were made by consultants on a less detailed basis, using interview and field data as the basis of their assessment.

7.   On the second visits the opportunity was taken to pass on brief details of the appraisal to those farmers who had requested further information. This second interview was not structured but simply followed the varying interests expressed by the farmers—again with a deliberately neutral approach. A note was taken of any changes in attitudes; of the type of advice sought; of prejudices regarding sources of advice, etc.

8.   **Forestry and Timber.** Each woodland was classified roughly according to its constitution ('coppice-with-standards', etc), and its general condition was assessed. Mensuration data was collected on a circular plot and angle count basis as laid down in the Forest Mensuration Handbook [25] and as advised by the Woodland Survey Team of the Forestry Commission's Research and Development Station. Particular note was taken of the distribution of species, diameter classes, and of any evidence (very infrequent) which might permit an assessment of yield class.

9.   Each wood was classified on a system worked out during the pilot study. This system attempts to give an indication both of the physical condition of a wood and its seral position. Volumes of timber were worked out from the mensuration data, using mainly the Forestry Commission's Tariff Tables [24] but sometimes Stand Tables (where stands were homogenous enough and sufficiently well stocked) and Form Heights. These were cross-checked on a sample basis and, on average, the Form Height method gave a 1.1 per cent greater estimate of timber volume than Stand Tables, and a 5.5 per cent greater estimate than the Tariff Tables. Coppice and other underwood was not assessed except where stems were consistently greater than 7 centimetres in diameter at a height of 1.6 metres.

10.   In order to appraise the value of the timber and other produce, discussions were held with timber merchants, mine timber agents, forestry contractors, and other buyers of standing timber in each area. The range of prices for standing timber and other produce, the level of demand for different species of produce, and an indication of the trends in demand were obtained, and the opportunity was taken to obtain their views on the quantities and qualities of supplies reaching them, and on apparent constraints on these supplies. As prices and conditions varied considerably from county to county, it meant that each wood had to be valued separately to obtain realistic figures.

11.   Attributing timber values was a difficult task: different valuations can be obtained depending on the purpose for which they are carried out. Thus a purchaser's valuation will normally be lower than a vendor's, and a valuation for Capital Transfer Tax will tend to be lower still. This is all part of a bargaining process. It is not sharp practice, there is merely a change in the underlying assumptions. Here each wood was taken on its merits, balancing the quality of the produce likely to be forthcoming against the calculated quantity of wood standing, species by species. Also taken into account were factors affecting access and harvesting: for example, the steepness or bogginess of ground, nearness to public and all-weather farm roads, etc. Thus a small wood located near a road with little in it to interest a timber merchant, might still command a price of sorts, but none if access was poor. Or, a small patch of scrub woodland might sell for charcoal in East Sussex, or for turnery poles in Gwent and Clwyd, but may be unsaleable in other counties. A demand for firewood (not always possible to check) was assumed but a firewood valuation was only placed on a wood as a marginal extra product from more lucrative felling (ie branchwood, tops and scrub-trees), or where a clear market existed and the quantity of wood (and easy access) justified it.

12.   A second problem concerned future management following the realisation of timber assets through felling. Except in the case of very small woods which contain less than 825 Hoppus feet and so need no felling licence*, there are some restrictions on the trees to be felled and also a licence might be granted only on condition of specific replanting. To take this into account would have meant assigning to each piece of woodland a set of constraints and replanting conditions reflecting fully the collective detailed policies of the local County Planning Office and the appropriate Conservancy of the Forestry Commission. This was clearly impossible, and any rule-of-thumb estimate would have been misleading. Therefore estimates of value were made on a clearfelling basis (an approach accepted by the Forestry Commission and the Royal Institution of Chartered Surveyors).

13.   Finally, the assignment of hypothetical produce values involved a good deal of subjective consideration, for instance in judging what proportion of mixed-age produce would be of planking quality, mining quality or pulpwood. This is inevitable in any timber valuation since a fine looking tree may well prove to be piped (or even hollow) on conversion. On the other hand, it seemed reasonable to assume that, where the external evidence supported it, a small percentage of the best stems of oak, ash, cherry and yew would be of veneer quality and this value was ascribed, with care, in appropriate circumstances. Detailed notes were taken of butt sweep, apparent stores (overgrown coppice shoots which are often prone to butt rot) diameter classes, species make-up, and so on. These notes, together with photographs, were used as a guide, but the estimates made from them can only be our best guess. If anything, we have erred on the conservative side, and they are probably best viewed as orders of magnitude.

14.   **Wildlife Conservation.** On the advice of the Nature Conservancy Council a simple assessment of the wildlife value of the woods was made using Peterken's method [58], amended in consultation with Dr Peterken. This is a count of vascular plants selected and listed as especially associated with woodland conditions. The rationale is that certain species of plant are indicative of long-established woodland cover and hence (on the theory of Island Biogeography) the woods where they are found have a higher value than less long-established woods. In addition, such plants are 'extinction prone', and the way their woodland habitats have been managed in the past, as well as their present condition, is essential to their survival. Beyond this, an attempt was made to classify the woods according to Peterken's Stand Types [62].

15.   It is important to note that the surveyors were not botanists and were only able to give this element of the survey limited time; also, counts had to be taken outside the months recommended by Peterken. Therefore, the counts obtained are probably underestimates. However, they were consistent within areas (and between survey teams when this was tested). The results are shown in the maps in Appendix II as simple 'scores'. This has the obvious drawback of not distinguishing between rare and common plants, but it does permit a close comparison of the value of the woods for wildlife *in any one area*. ('Score' comparisons between study areas are quite meaningless.)

---

*Under the *Forestry Act 1949*, IX, Part II (4) (1), up to 825 cu ft (Hoppus) (29.75 cu m) may be felled for the owner's personal use in any quarter. Thus a wood containing less than this amount of standing timber may be felled in one operation without a licence. Slightly larger woods can be felled *seriatim* over several quarters. However, only 25 per cent of the produce may be sold off the holding.

16. **Landscape.** The landscape significance of the woodlands in each study area was related to:

    i.   topography and land use;

    ii.   access by road and on foot;

    iii. the different groups of people likely to view the landscape;

    iv. the size, appearance and location of the woods;

    v.   the relationship of the woods to hedgerows and other landscape features.

17. **The Woods.** The woods in the study areas were classified into one of the three following groups:

    i.   Woods of visual importance—those visible to the greatest number of people but not necessarily of the greatest visual beauty (predominantly located on the horizon or on slopes facing roads or well-populated areas).

    ii.   Woods of landscape importance—those which formed part of the overall landscape but were not necessarily visually important.

    iii. Woods which were neither conspicuous nor of landscape importance.

18. **Game.** The game consultant took into account four factors in his assessment of the value of woods:

    i.   The climatic and topographical nature of the area including, of course, its size, location and the condition of its woods;

    ii.   the size of farm holdings, individual fields, and the prevailing agricultural enterprises;

    iii. the interest or lack of interest in game conservation noted by the surveyors during the first interviews;

    iv. any existing shooting in the area.

19. **History.** Due to pressures of time, this aspect of the research was confined to establishing the changes which had taken place in the actual ground area covered by woodland. The assessment was based on evidence on the ground and verbal evidence, supplemented by a comparison with the reproductions.(David and Charles) of the First Edition ('Old Series') 1-inch Ordnance Survey maps (originally published over the period 1801 to 1873). In some cases, evidence was obtained from aerial photographs, but no comprehensive examination of these was attempted, nor were archival sources checked. There are often errors in the First Edition Ordnance Survey maps (remarked on by Rackham [63] and by Dickinson [16]) but they were readily available and were thought to be indicative, at least, of an historical trend in woodland cover.

20. In addition, there were indications of woodland origins and former functions, (and of the types of management and species favoured) in the names of woods and fields—for example references to 'Copse' and 'Plantation'; to 'Kilns', 'Guns' and 'Powder'; to events such as 'Victoria Jubilee'—and also in the shapes of woodland boundaries. From this and from verbal evidence came some sort of picture of the history of the woods in relation to their former markets.

Appendix II

The Case Studies

Introduction

1. The areas studied are taken by county in alphabetical order. A broadly similar format is used for each area, as follows:

   i. **Landscape:**
       a. roads, rivers and other relevant topographical features;

       b. boundaries;

       c. access;

       d. areas of woodland, farmland, etc.

   ii. **Agriculture:**
       a. sizes and ownership of farms;

       b. types of agriculture typical of the area.

   iii. **The Farmers:**
       a. woodland ownership;

       b. attitudes to woods and conservation;
       c. evidence of present woodland activity.

   iv. **The Woods:**
       a. distribution and area;

       b. changes in woodland cover;

       c. markets and demand for produce;

       d. physical condition;

       e. wildlife appraisal;

       f. forestry and timber appraisal;

       g. game appraisal.

   v. **Conclusions and Prognosis.**

2. With nine areas to describe, we have had to cover a lot of ground very concisely. In particular, the quantitative material has been aggregated and cross-comparisons have been largely omitted. This conciseness and aggregation also stems from the need to observe a high degree of confidentiality. A good deal of concern was expressed by a high proportion of farmers and land-owners (and by timber processors in respect of prices etc) that they were subjected to considerably prying into their affairs, and it was only by promising to observe a high degree of confidentiality in reporting the research that their co-operation was achieved. In particular, we have taken great care to avoid identifying any particular farm or estate or any one wood. Only the plant 'scores' are identified for individual woods, these being of specialist interest and unrelated to the life or economy of a farm. As in the rest of the report the tabulated percentages are rounded to the nearest whole number and so some columns do not total exactly 100 per cent.

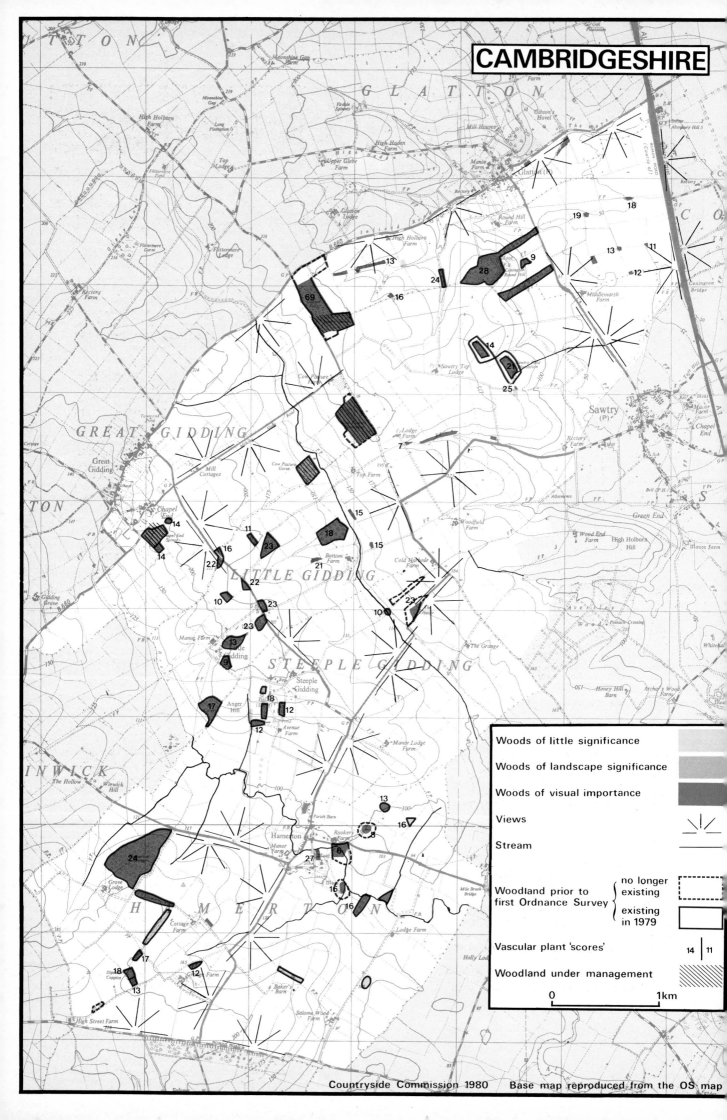

CAMBRIDGESHIRE

Woods of little significance

Woods of landscape significance

Woods of visual importance

Views

Stream

Woodland prior to first Ordnance Survey
- no longer existing
- existing in 1979

Vascular plant 'scores' 14 | 11

Woodland under management

0   1km

Countryside Commission 1980   Base map reproduced from the OS map

Cambridgeshire

Landscape

A.1 The study area in Cambridgeshire, a county of high quality soils and intensive farming, is one of the few districts left in the county which still have some vestige of woodland. It consists of flat or softly rolling countryside with large arable fields and few buildings outside the villages. Three streams run roughly west to east across the area. The boundaries taken were the A1 on the north-east side, the A604 to the south, the B660 to the north-west, and unclassified roads, a stream and field boundaries to the east and west. The map shows these boundaries and something of the landscape structure of the area.

A.2 In all there are some eleven villages and hamlets in the area or on the periphery, and they are linked by a number of good minor roads. The area is also close to larger settlements, being approximately twelve kilometres from the centre of Peterborough, ten kilometres from Huntingdon, and twenty-three kilometres from Bedford. The roads are for the most part straight, without hedges, so views of the countryside are easily obtained, as the frequency of viewpoints on the Map shows. In this open landscape woods are a dominant feature and a softening element.

A.3 Its 3,379 hectares make it one of the largest of the nine study areas. Its size is due to the need to cover an adequate cross-section of farmers and landowners (and woods) in a locality of large land-holdings. There are 74.9 hectares of woods (just over 2 per cent of the total land area), of which 58.6 hectares are unmanaged. Table A.1 shows the size and ownership of the holdings; the large size of most farms is evident—two being over 400 hectares. Estate-owned woodlands are, however, mostly 'in hand'.

Table A.1 Size and Ownership of Farms in the Cambridgeshire Study Area

	20 ha & below	21–40 ha	41–60 ha	61–80 ha	81–100 ha	Over 100 ha
Number of farms	2	1	1	1	1	7
Proportion of total (Base 13) (Owner-occupiers[1] 6) (Tenants[1] 9) (Refusals 2) (No-contact 4)	15%	8%	8%	8%	8%	54%

[1]Farmers may both own and rent land in the area

A.4 The geology of the area is very simple, with Jurassic Oxford Clays over the whole area, overlain with Boulder Clay drifts running roughly north-west to south-east. The soils are deep heavy clays which, after careful drainage, give Class 2 agricultural land. Roughly two-thirds of the farmland appears to be used for cereals, with the other third under grass ley or crops such as oil seed rape. However, sugar beet, potatoes and beans are also grown, and beef cattle and sheep are raised. It is a very intensively farmed area, cultivated right up to well-maintained deep drains and fences.

The Farmers

A.5 Nineteen farmers had holdings in the area. Interviews were obtained with thirteen, two of whom had no woods. Also interviewed were the agent managing one of the three big estates in the area and the gamekeeper-cum-forester for another (on the recommendation of the London-based agent). Six farmers and the gamekeeper-cum-forester were interviewed a second time. Woods on the estates are managed principally for pheasant shooting, although some timber has been removed—mainly dead elm. Additionally, 14.3 hectares of existing woodland have been felled and replanted, mainly with conifers, conifer and hardwood mixtures, or hybrid poplars. The new areas have been planted over the last twelve years. Two other owners use their woods for rearing game, and another four value them for their game-holding function but do not rear birds.

A.6 The attitudes of farmers, owners, the agents and the keeper are mixed, but generally sympathetic and occasionally enthusiastic. Most of the tenant farmers feel that financial gain is not applicable since the woods are not theirs.

Table A.2 Attitudes to Woods in the Cambridgeshire Study Area*

	Woods/trees in general	Landscape	Wildlife	Game	Financial gain/loss
Strongly interested/ appreciative/anxious	6	6	3	6	3
Quite interested/ appreciative/anxious	6	4	5	5	—
Mildly interested/ appreciative/anxious	1	2	1	—	1
Indifferent	2	2	4	2	7
Antipathetic	—	—	—	—	—
Inapplicable	—	—	—	2	5

A.7 A number of the respondents were interested in doing more with their woods. Some advice was sought on grants but others rejected the idea ("too many conditions", "too much paperwork", "our responsibility, not government's", etc) and were willing to consider putting things to rights if that were thought proper by someone more knowledgeable on the subject. One owner treats his woods as an extension of his garden—family working picnics, collecting acorns (used for raising oak plants in his garden for replanting), planting and weeding.

The Woods

A.8 The woods are distributed as shown on the Map. The smallest tend to be on wetter patches or around small ponds. There are a number of tree belts, perhaps planted for game management (although the game consultant thought not). The larger woods are in blocks. Few woods are named, but 'Gorse' and 'Grove' in two or three cases each could indicate some modest antiquity and natural origins relative to the 'Plantation' and 'Coppice' names which also appear. They were divided by ownership and (rarely) stand type, into 73 woods (five holdings of 20, 13, 10, 6 and 5 woods each; two with 4 woods; one with 3 woods; three with 2 woods; and two with only 1 wood), of which the 59 unmanaged woods, or parts of woods, were surveyed.

A.9 Compared to the old series Ordnance Survey map there is little difference apparent in tree cover. The old map shows approximately 70 hectares of woods although it seems quite likely that a number may have been too small to plot on a one-inch map. Thus over the last 100 to 160 years the woodlands appear to have remained quite stable. Evidence suggests that in the past they were largely managed as coppice, but with significant old plantations of elm. It is impossible on the little evidence immediately available to speculate on the traditional markets for their produce. Present-day markets are fair to good for most of the species found. (Because of the very good road system and the Midlands location the market for quality hardwoods appears to be excellent). The main market is for general purpose saw milling with numerous saw-mills within a forty kilometre radius. However, markets for bulk quantities of low-grade timber are non-existent. There was reported to be an adequate number of forestry and timber contractors in the vicinity.

A.10 There are interesting contrasts in the physical condition of the woods; with the smaller ones looking neglected (partly by reason of so much dead elm) and larger woods being reasonably well looked after, with paths kept clear, some new planting at the edges, and dead trees having been removed. Growth of newly planted trees is good, with hardwood growth matching (and in some cases surpassing) its conifer nurse. However, natural regeneration is mostly scanty, woodland floors bare, and mature trees dying or moribund. Hares and rabbits are abundant and may be keeping seedlings down. (There is some control of a number of predators for game rearing reasons: this may have to be increased if the game potential is to be fully realised).

Fine young elm in grave danger from Dutch elm disease

*It was not always possible to ascribe attitudes, so the bases in these tables may vary and may be less than the total sample.

Table A.3 Areas of Woods Surveyed in the Cambridgeshire Study Area

	Number of woods	Proportion of total (Base 59)
Less than 0.25 ha	30	51%
0.26 ha to 1 ha	17	29%
1.01 ha to 5 ha	9	15%
5.01 ha to 9.9 ha	2	3%
10 ha and over	1	2%

A.11 **Wildlife.** There is no clear 'stand type' (as in the Nature Conservancy classification [62]) into which the woods fall—possibly because of introductions and because many woods are old plantations, for instance on old 'rig and furrow'. The level of vascular plant scores, with one exception, is not high, but that might be expected with small isolated pieces of woodland. Plants associated with old woodlands were identified, particularly on the wetter areas, and, in the Cambridgeshire context at least, the woods do have a clear value for wildlife.

Table A.4 Types of Woodland in the Cambridgeshire Study Area

		Number	Proportion
A.	Recently planted woodlands	14	19%
B.	Scrub woodland invasion	2	3%
C.	Secondary regrowth on areas clearfelled 30 to 40 years ago	—	—
D.	Self-sown woods of mixed age trees and shrubs	6	8%
E.	Coppice wood with few and poor standards	12	16%
F.	Overgrown coppice with standards and 'stores'	13	18%
G.	Woods and parks of mature trees with no natural regeneration	9	12%
H.	Areas recently clearfelled but no new planting	2	3%
I.	Mature/semi-mature plantations (may have admixture of natural regeneration and coppice)	15	20%
J.	High forest of native spp. (may have a few planted exotics)	—	—
K.	Coppice/coppice-with-standards in good condition	—	—
		(Base 73)	

A.12 **Forestry and Timber.** Table A.4 shows something of the physical condition of the woods. There is interest in forestry management evident (or the intention expressed) on the estate-owned land, and nearly a fifth of the total woodland has been newly planted—albeit occasionally with species which are not too well suited to the site and which are game-orientated in choice (eg spruce). There are sufficient examples of good standards to demonstrate the suitability of the area for growing quality timber: valuations are shown in Table A.5. The estimated volume of standing timber in the unmanaged woods (exclud-

Table A.5 Quantities and Values of Forest Produce

Type of produce	Species	Quantity[1] (cu.m)	Standing value (£)
Sawlogs	Oak	430	6,611
	Ash	460	18,997
	Sycamore	64	804
	Elm	5,777	149,814
	Poplar	27	111
	Field Maple	8	31
	Scots Pine	9	44
	Norway Spruce	23	187
	Yew	1	69
	Sawlog totals	6,799	176,668
Firewood		7,444 tonnes[2]	3,724
	GRAND TOTAL		£180,392

[1]Rounded to nearest whole cubic metre
[2]Green weight

ing hazel coppice and shrubs) totalled in round terms 11,644 cubic metres with a total value of £180,392. This approximates to £3,078 per hectare, or £15.49 per cubic metre. However, this valuation is dominated by one outstanding wood: if this were to be excluded, then the averages would be reduced (again in round terms) to 102 cubic metres per hectare, £771 per hectare, and £7.55 per cubic metre. Twenty-eight of the smaller woods have no standing value whatever.

A.13 **Game.** This was once predominantly a partridge shooting area, but more intensive farming and the removal of many hedgerows have greatly reduced the partridge population, so that pheasants are now the only game bird with management potential. Although such management as the woods receive is game-orientated, paradoxically, as hedgerows have been removed, their importance for game cover has increased. Since Dutch elm disease is now transforming the woods (with major losses still to come), and since many woodlands are bare and draughty for want of adequate management in the past, many owners are going to encounter serious problems in the near future.

A.14 Although demand in the area is high, shooting quality is not what it could be, and unless measures are taken it will deteriorate for the reasons given above. The potential for game conservation is therefore difficult to assess, and its successful promotion would be dependent both on restoring existing woods and establishing some new ones. However, there is some room for improvement through better planning and management, and, because of the ready demand for sporting rights, it could be economically attractive.

Conclusion

A.15 The woods in the Cambridgeshire study area are in physical decline, which is being exacerbated by Dutch elm disease. Relative to some of the areas examined they have been quite stable in size, shape and location over a century or so, and the reason they have not suffered the fate of the area's hedgerows is at least partly because of their value for game. There appears to be no danger of them being deliberately removed but, because of the lack of natural regeneration (or vigorous coppice re-growth), they could gradually disappear over the next few decades. What is more likely to happen is that they will be cut and replanted with conifers or conifer and broadleaved mixtures (or, in some cases, with widely spaced hybrid poplar), which will result in some change in the landscape in the medium and long term.

A.16 There is urgent need for multi-purpose management advice on conserving and restoring these woodlands. With the larger woods, there would be some useful cash flow from harvesting operations, but for most others such work could not be paid for in this way and they will require new investment. However, such investment may well yield extra dividends in the form of improved shooting and possibly higher rents.

Clwyd

Landscape

B.1   The study area, part of the Vale of Clwyd, was selected because it is typical of much of the fertile lowlands of Wales—a long alluvial valley carved out of the surrounding steep uplands—and for the contrasts it provides between valley woods and woods in the higher re-entrant (or tributary) valleys above. The area chosen covers a section of the valley between the eastern watershed and the valley bottom. The western boundary was set as the A525 (Wrexham–St Asaph–Rhyl) road which runs north and south along the valley and, due to its slightly raised position, gives panoramic views of the river, its valley farms and the slopes and re-entrant valleys to the east. The Offa's Dyke long-distance footpath, which runs along the edge of the valley scarp, was chosen as the eastern boundary, while to the north and south the boundaries are the A541 (Denbigh to Mold) road and the A494 (Queensferry to Dolgellau) trunk road.

B.2   The Vale of Clwyd is twenty-five kilometres from the Snowdonia National Park and about the same distance from the North Wales coast. Parts of the towns of Denbigh and Ruthin are within the study area, as are some seven or eight hamlets. The area is thus probably the most 'public' of any examined in the study. It is certainly the most spectacular, whether seen from Offa's Dyke or from the boundary roads. The Map shows the landscape features and the significant viewpoints into and within the area. As the Map shows, the area is densely packed with small fields, the smaller and more irregular of which are probably pre-enclosure, with a sudden change to moorland common at the break of the slope to the hills alongside. There is a considerable density of minor roads serving hamlets and farms from the spinal B5429. The landscape importance of the woods was a little difficult to establish. The little remaining woodland in the re-entrant valleys is plain to the eye but, even with the aid of a map and from the ridge above, it is difficult to see the lower valley woods amongst the numerous hedgerow trees. However, they are an important part of the micro-landscape within the area. The area covers approximately 4,513 hectares. Only 45.3 hectares of woodland were noted, of which 39 are unmanaged. Settlements cover approximately 70 hectares, and the remainder is farmland. Table B.1 shows the variety of farm sizes found.

Table B.1   Size and Ownership of Farms in the Clwyd Study Area

	20 ha & below	21–40 ha	41–60 ha	61–80 ha	81–100 ha	Over 100 ha
Number of farms	5	5	3	1	1	3
Proportion of total	28%	28%	17%	6%	6%	17%

(Base 19)
(Owner-occupiers[1]   12)
(Tenants[1]   8)
(Information refused 1)
(Interview Refused   2)
(No contact—unquantifiable)

[1]Farmers may both own and rent land in the area

B.3   The basic geology of the area is fairly simple, with Triassic sandstones forming east and west slopes above the alluvium, and Silurian shales forming the hills to the east. In the south-west the area touches Carboniferous limestone beyond the Llanrhaiadr Fault. There are overlying glacial deposits of Pebble Beds, Boulder Clay, 'outwash' sands and gravels and, of course, the alluvium of the valley bottom. The alluvial soils are rich and constitute much of the little Class 1 agricultural land in North Wales. Higher, the soils are acid, sandy loams of fair depth—good Class 2 land; higher still are shallow acid soils on shale. The farming is very mixed, with dairying, beef and sheep rearing, cereals and fodder crops. Pig and poultry production was also noted. A number of the farms also have sheep grazing rights on the common hill land of the Clwydian range.

The Farmers

B.4   Due to the need to cover a reasonable number and area of woodland, the final area chosen contained too big a population of farmers to reach them all within the available time and money. Over fifty of the 100-plus farmers in the area were contacted by telephone. They were asked if they had woods on their holdings; if the reply was positive an interview was requested. A total of nineteen farmers were interviewed. Another refused an interview but permitted access to his woods, two refused altogether, and a third changed his mind and refused access to his woods after the interview. Because of the rather hidden nature of the valley woods, it is not certain that the 45.3 hectares noted above includes all the woods in the area, but most were certainly included and the only major omissions would be those woods being brought under management by an owner whom it was not possible to contact.

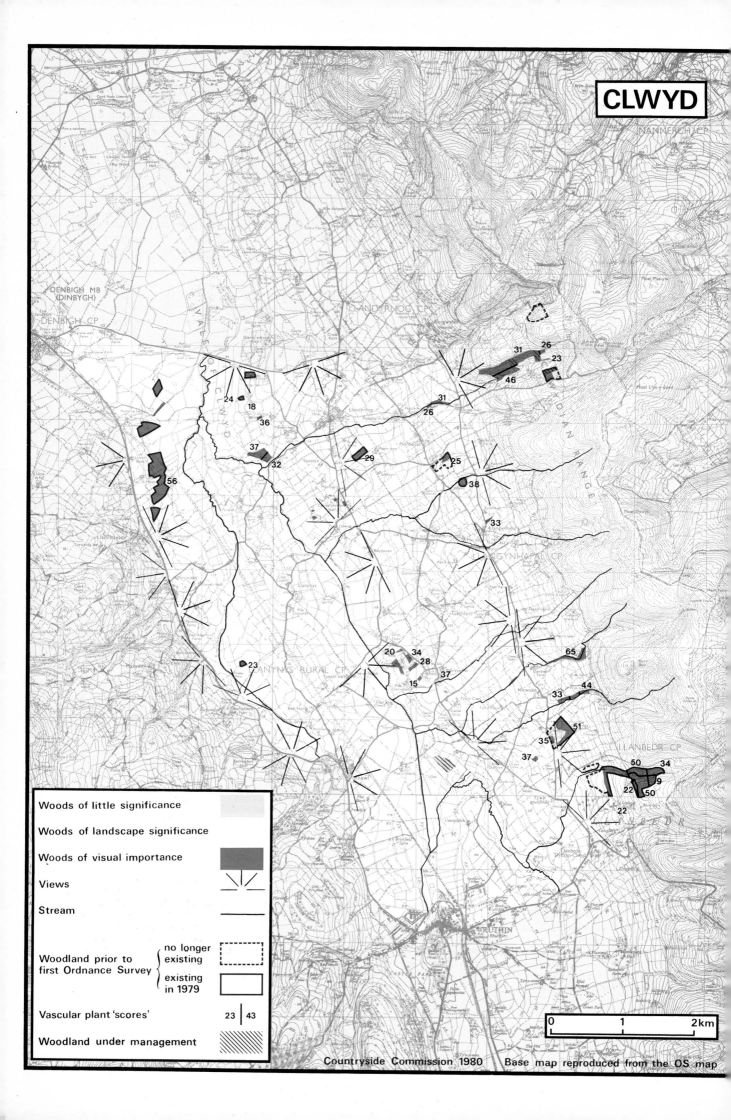

CLWYD

Legend

Woods of little significance

Woods of landscape significance

Woods of visual importance

Views

Stream

Woodland prior to first Ordnance Survey
- no longer existing
- existing in 1979

Vascular plant 'scores'   23 | 43

Woodland under management

Countryside Commission 1980   Base map reproduced from the OS map

0   1   2km

B.5   As well as the mixed farming of the area there is also an interesting mixture of types of farmer from the very business-like, farming with considerably intensity (and slowly removing hedges and reclaiming woodland to do so), to the very conservative, practising an older form of management. Of the nineteen interviewed, one is bringing his woods under management, using mainly conifers but with species and group shapes planted in a very careful way and in sympathy with the landscape. Four others have planted trees, either to thicken up woods or in new locations (around a pond, for example), but have been disappointed at their lack of success. Alder woods on two tenant farms are held 'in hand' by the owner (whom it was not possible to speak to), and one of these has been partly felled and replanted with hybrid poplar. Five respondents have cleared woodland at some time in the past, and one intends to clear about 1.2 hectares in the near future. One tenant would like the woods (mainly alder) on his farm cleared for agriculture. Woods are used for occasional firewood, gateposts, etc, and most are grazed at least periodically. Ten farmers asked for a second interview with the DART forester.

B.6   Attitudes are summarised in Table B.2. Appreciation of woodland, which in several cases has gone as far as action, is fairly high for woods with a (personal) amenity, landscape, or wildlife function, but is lower for game. On the question of financial gain, opinion is more evenly divided:

Table B.2   Attitudes to Woods in the Clwyd Study Area

	Woods/trees in general	Landscape	Wildlife	Game	Financial gain/loss
Strongly interested/ appreciative/anxious	6	6	5	—	3
Quite interested/ appreciative/anxious	9	10	11	6	6
Mildly interested/ appreciative/anxious	1	1	1	2	1
Indifferent	2	2	2	8	8
Antipathetic	1	—	—	2	—
Inapplicable	—	—	—	1	1

During second interviews, most respondents asked about grants, and three asked for more detailed management advice (in at least one case, probably, more to check the interviewer's credentials than out of real interest).

The Woods

B.7   The distribution of the woods is shown on the Map: they fall into three broad categories. First, there are those lying in the lower sides and bottoms of the re-entrant valleys—possibly remnants of former native sessile oak forest in two cases, or wood-land invasion earlier this century in others. Second, there are fairly obvious old plantations of larch, ash, beech, sycamore and sweet chestnut. Third, there are woods of very mixed character on wet ground—alder mainly, but lime, birch, ash, cherry, rowan, field maple, willow and the more usual shrubs. Divided by ownership and stand type there are some 45 woods, of which four are being managed. One farmer has 8 woods; one has 6; one has 4; three have 3 each; five have 2 and eight have 1 wood. Table B.3 shows the size distribution of the unmanaged woods.

Table B.3   Areas of Woods Surveyed in the Clwyd Study Area

	Number of woods	Proportion of total (Base 40)
Less than 0.25 ha	9	22%
0.26 ha to 1 ha	18	45%
1.01 ha to 5 ha	12	30%
5.01 ha to 9.9 ha	1	2%
10 ha and over	—	—

B.8   Comparison with the old series Ordnance Survey maps was particularly difficult because of the intensity of hachuring used for hilly areas on these maps, but there has probably been a reduction of approximately 31 per cent in woodland area since the early surveys. The traditional management of the hill woods was probably as oak coppice, latterly with an admixture of exotic species including larch, Scots pine and sycamore. The wet-ground woods were probably also coppiced. Most of the produce was used locally, perhaps in the numerous mines and quarries further west. Heavy felling took place during the two World Wars, as reported by older farmers and from the evidence of the rotting butts. One farmer also spoke of heavy felling during the 1930s. All feelings appear to have been of plantation conifers, oak and ash. Present markets for sawlogs are good. with the industrial north-west within easy reach and needing a range of products. There is also a pulpwood market (but for softwoods only) and a market for turnery poles. There are two hardwood saw-mills on the margins of the study area, and three more within twenty kilometres.

B.9   As the Map shows, access to the woods is reasonable, owing to their proximity to roads, although hill woods are difficult to reach, and this and the cost of operating machinery on boggy ground near the river would be adverse factors. There are enough contractors in the area. Tree growth-rates vary from fairly good in the valley to slow higher up the slopes. There is evidence of stunted growth caused by the winds funnelled through the area when southerly or northerly gales blow. Table B.4 shows the general types of woodland found.

Table B.4   Types of Woodland in the Clwyd Study Area

		Number	*Proportion*
A.	Recently planted woodlands	4	9%
B.	Scrub woodland invasion	2	4%
C.	Secondary regrowth on areas clearfelled 30 to 40 years ago	3	7%
D.	Self-sown woods of mixed age trees and shrubs	8	18%
E.	Coppice wood with few and poor standards	3	7%
F.	Overgrown coppice with standards and 'stores'	12	27%
G.	Woods and parks of mature trees with no natural regeneration	12	27%
H.	Areas recently clearfelled but no new planting	1	2%
I.	Mature/semi-mature plantations (may have admixture of natural regeneration and coppice)	—	—
J.	High forest of native spp. (may have a few planted exotics)	—	—
K.	Coppice/coppice-with-standards in good condition	—	—

(Base 45)

B.10   **Wildlife.** The woods in the area have been so altered by past management and use that they are difficult to classify in Nature Conservancy Council Stand Types [62]. For the re-entrant valley woods, they probably come nearest to the upland hazel-sessile oakwood type, whilst the wetter woods on the alluvial soil are acid alderwoods and bird-cherry alderwoods. The Map shows the plant scores. The highest number of listed plants was found in a re-entrant valley wood not shown on the old Ordnance Survey map but, like the Gwent examples quoted later, it seems likely that this wood is of a substantial age. In general, the wetwoods of the valley bottom and the re-entrant woods have the highest value for wildlife, any former plantations scoring consistently lower. In this moist, western climate, even relatively small woods can continue to support an interesting plant mosaic.

B.11   **Forestry and Timber.** These woodlands, with the exception of the ones being brought under management (paragraph B.5), are in a very poor state, long-established grazing having reduced many to a park-like fringe around a better-stocked, over-mature centre. The effect of this over time can clearly be seen from the former outlines on the Map. Oak regeneration has suffered in particular and, although the stumps of large oaks are evident in many woods, there are now very few oak standards. It seems likely that, in this small area at least, the 'Welsh Oak' of the old timber trade may well become extinct. Ash and sycamore regeneration appears a little more robust but is not profuse; only alder appears to hold its own. Table B.5 summarises the valuations placed on the woods in the area. The total standing volume of wood in the unmanaged woods was estimated to be 4,437 cubic metres, or 114 cubic metres per hectare. The average values were estimated at £875 per hectare and £7.67 per cubic metre.

Useful stand of mature oak, but open to stock grazing

B.12   **Game.** Almost uniquely in North Wales, there is considerable small-scale shooting in the Vale of Clwyd, with several moderately sized (mostly syndicated) pheasant shooting estates, and numerous syndicates of local residents which shoot partridge, duck, woodcock, rabbit and hare, as well as pheasant. There have been small syndicates of local farmers within the area in the past, but they have broken up because (partly through their informality) some individuals found themselves doing all the work. Climatically the Vale is suitable for both game husbandry and the cultivation of a suitable mix of agricultural crops which are helpful to game. Wind is a major problem, particularly north-westerlies. If the woods were to be improved and enlarged, there would be a significant amelioration. There is some interest in game conservation, both outside and inside the

Table B.5 Quantities and Values of Forest Produce

Type of produce	Species	Quantity[1] (cu m)	Standing Value (£)
Sawlogs	Oak	353	9,548
	Ash	295	7,491
	Beech	147	1,755
	Sycamore	351	4,628
	Elm	138	1,845
	Sweet Chestnut	82	1,441
	Alder	220	610
	Cherry	49	3,510
	Lime	10	57
	Larch	30	342
	Sawlog totals	1,676	31,227
Turnery Billets (Yew)		50 tonnes[2]	500
Turnery Poles		365 tonnes[2]	650
Firewood		3,340 tonnes[2]	1,671
		GRAND TOTAL	£34,048

[1] Rounded to nearest whole cubic metre
[2] Green weight

study area, but the small size of holdings means that there would have to be co-operation between farmers and landowners, which would need to be on an agreed practical and administrative footing.

Conclusion

B.13   Despite the strong sympathies felt for woodlands by many farmers, the area's woodlands are under pressure. In the first place, it seems very likely that, as in other areas of Class 1 agricultural land, the woods on flatter ground will eventually be cleared for agriculture. Hedges are already being cleared, and there has been a marked rise in land prices, which for new entrants to farming is bound to add to the pressures for clearance. Even farmers who are planting more trees (or thinking of doing so) appear for the most part to be under the impression that new groups of trees are fair exchange for old: ie they appear to be sensitive to the landscape aspects but not to wildlife. Second, many woods in the area—particularly on the drier slopes—are especially vulnerable to agricultural use for grazing and shelter. Yet the goodwill is there to alter this situation for the better, if some of the obvious financial problems can be overcome.

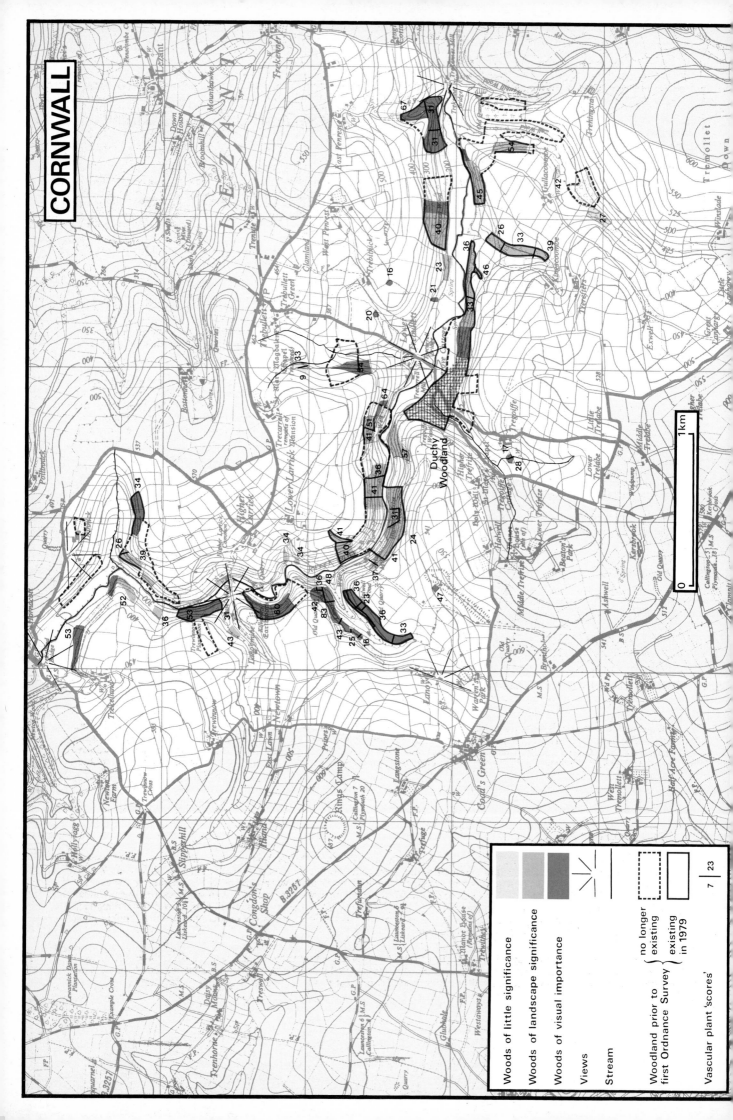

CORNWALL

Woods of little significance

Woods of landscape significance

Woods of visual importance

Views

Stream

Woodland prior to first Ordnance Survey { no longer existing / existing in 1979 }

Vascular plant 'scores'

7 | 23

1km

Duchy Woodland

Cornwall

Landscape

C.1   The study area in Cornwall was selected as being typical of wooded areas in East Cornwall and Devon generally. It consists of steep, wooded slopes on either side of a 5.5 kilometre stretch of the River Inny, with fields on the flattened hilltops above and meadows, often narrow, between woods and river. The boundaries of the study area were set as the B3257 and a minor road running roughly parallel to the river; and the B3254 and a minor road which roughly mark the boundary between the mainly unmanaged woods of the valley farms and the professionally managed estate woodlands to the east and west (see Map).

C.2   Two other roads run through the valley and there is a fairly complex system of county and private roads serving the small hamlets and the nineteen farms within the area. The roads are narrow and winding, with high banks and hedges on each side, so that views of the countryside beyond are only obtainable at field gates and road intersections. Even then, the convexity of the upper slopes reduces vision into the valley itself to a very occasional glimpse, except where roads actually cross the river to reveal vistas of sorts. It is an enclosed, almost secret, valley, some six kilometres from Launceston, away from the mainstream of Cornish tourism.

C.3   The study area covers 1,280 hectares. There are 74 hectares of woodland, of which some 12 hectares are being managed (and therefore were excluded from the field survey). The remainder is almost entirely agricultural. Table C.1 shows the pattern of farm size to be very variable:

Table C.1   Size and Ownership of Farms in the Cornwall Study Area

	20 ha & below	21–40 ha	41–60 ha	61–80 ha	81–100 ha	Over 100 ha
Number of farms	4	5	4	2	3	1
Proportion of total	21%	26%	21%	11%	16%	5%

(Base 19)
(Owner-occupiers[1]   13)
(Tenants[1]   6)
(Refusals   1)

[1]Farmers may both own and rent land in the area

The geology of the area is complex, with igneous rocks alternating with sedimentary and metamorphosed rocks (shales and grits, chert, slate and thin limestone). The soils are acid and shallow, and so the area consists mainly of lower Class 3 agricultural land, with some Class 4 land on the steeper slopes. Farming is mixed, with beef, dairying, sheep, cereals, potatoes and feed crops, and is mainly traditional in character with few new buildings or heavy machines, and little or no hedge removal amongst the small fields.

The Farmers

C.4   Of the nineteen farmers with holdings in the area, only one has no woodlands. None refused a first interview. One farmer is in the process of felling his woods for replanting (with conifers after Forestry Commission advice and a possible Small Woods Grant). The woods on three tenanted farms are retained 'in hand' by the landowners, one of whom had cleared the existing woodland and replanted with conifers some years previously, while the owner of the other two farms carries out no active management but permits one interested tenant to do a little clearing of dead trees, etc. The remaining fourteen do not manage their existing woods in any way, although one has recently planted up a field corner. Some produce (mainly firewood) is taken for their own use. Thirteen farmers were interviewed a second time.

C.5   The farmers are generally sympathetic in their attitudes to woodlands (as Table C.2 indicates); indeed, three of them were thinking of planting up other areas. One farmer liked woods, but not on his own farm, and two more felt that woods should only occupy ground unusable for agriculture. Two appreciative farmers felt that their woods "ought to pay their way":

Table C.2 Attitudes to Woods in the Cornwall Study Area

	Woods/trees in general	Landscape	Wildlife	Game	Financial gain/loss
Strongly interested/ appreciative/anxious	6	5	3	1	5
Quite interested/ appreciative/anxious	9	10	5	2	6
Mildly interested/ appreciative/anxious	3	3	6	4	3
Indifferent	1	—	4	9	5
Antipathetic	—	1	1	3	—

In general, they are aware of the shortcomings in their approaches to their woods: a lack of time and money to some extent but, above all, a lack of practical and detailed advice. A high proportion are avid for information and frequently held the interviewer in long discussions.

The Woods

C.6 The distribution of the woods can be seen on the Map. Most lie along the main valley sides and in the re-entrant valleys. As separate pieces of woodland they number 30, but categorised by ownership and stand type for field surveys (and again excluding those under management) there are 64 woods altogether. One farm has 1 wood; four farms have 2 woods, nine farms have 3 woods; two farms have 4 woods; one farm has 5 woods and one farm has 15 woods.

Table C.3 Areas of Woods Surveyed in the Cornwall Study Area

	Number of woods	Proportion of total (Base 63)
Less than 0.25 ha	17	27%
0.26 ha to 1 ha	22	35%
1.01 ha to 5 ha	22	35%
5.01 ha to 9.9 ha	2	3%
10 ha and over	—	

C.7 Checked against the old series Ordnance Survey maps the area of woodland appears to have been reduced by about 42 per cent over the last 150 years or so. The survey evidence suggests that the traditional management was as oak coppice but, with the admixture of beech and some conifers in the late nineteenth century, a proportion were converted to a type of high forest management. Traditional markets were probably for tan bark, mining timbers and charcoal for the smelters. Of these local markets, only the one for tan bark was reported still to exist (Cornwall has one of the last remaining tanneries which use oak bark for tanning, and it was their hides which were used for the replica of St Brendan's boat which recently made a successful crossing of the Atlantic [65]). However, no tan bark had been taken from the area within the memory of the respondents.

C.8 The present main local market is for general-purpose saw-milling, with five small mills in Cornwall (three powered from a stationary agricultural tractor) which cut local hardwoods, but only in very small quantities. Some bulk hardwoods may be taken by a large chipboard factory at South Molton in Devon. Good timber-sized oak, ash and chestnut were reported to be in wide demand regionally (and nationally), and such a stand would attract buyers from well beyond the Tamar. There are also signs of a developing firewood market, with offers on a per acre basis for clearfelling recently having been received by two farmers just outside the area. However, local demand for some species (particularly sycamore) is non-existent.

C.9 The narrow valleys, the lack of roads, and the steep slopes make access difficult. This together with the small size of the local saw-mill industry makes prices for standing timber in the area very low compared with the other areas studied. An additional difficulty mentioned by estate agents and two saw-millers is a shortage of good contractors for felling, extracting and transporting to the mills. This is also true for purely forestry work: one respondent could find no one interested in a two-year contract for low-pruning plantations.

C.10 Tree and plant growth in the area is locally luxuriant, but there is considerable evidence of slow deterioration, due mainly to grazing by holding stock especially in wet and cold weather. One respondent stated that his woods are saving him a capital sum of £15,000 on erecting buildings which would otherwise be necessary. Table C.4 indicates the physical character of the woods. There is also cause for concern at the degree of canopy closure and its effect on ground flora, but the high light intensities found in Cornwall makes this less serious than in more northerly areas.

Table C.4 Types of Woodland in the Cornwall Study Area

		Number	Proportion
A.	Recently planted woodlands	1	2%
B.	Scrub woodland invasion	3	5%
C.	Secondary regrowth on areas clearfelled 30 to 40 years ago	5	8%
D.	Self-sown woods of mixed age trees and shrubs	12	19%
E.	Coppice wood with few and poor standards	7	11%
F.	Overgrown coppice with standards and 'stores'	17	27%
G.	Woods and parks of mature trees with no natural regeneration	17	27%
H.	Areas recently clearfelled but no new planting	2	3%
I.	Mature/semi-mature plantations (may have admixture of natural regeneration and coppice)	—	—
J.	High forest of native spp. (may have a few planted exotics)	—	—
K.	Coppice/coppice-with-standards in good condition	—	—

(Base 64)

(In addition, there are woodlands managed under Forestry Commission Dedication Schemes, excluded from survey.)

C.11 **Wildlife.** Insofar as it is possible to classify the woods, using the Nature Conservancy Council's Stand Types [62], they belong mainly to the ash-hazel and acid birch-oakwoods groups, with some alderwoods on wetter areas. On the evidence of the plant counts shown on the Map, they are of high wildlife value, with one-third scoring over 40. Several woods show evidence of badgers. There is no clear relationship between the type of woodland (Table C.4 above) and the plant scores, except for the one newly-planted plot which scored only 9. The average score for woods in categories F and G (those throwing the heaviest shade) is 36 and 34 respectively. However, there is a noticeable reduction in the score of category G woods which are heavily grazed, with typical values of 20 to 30.

C.12 **Forestry and Timber.** From a forester's viewpoint, the woodlands are in a bad condition. In spite of stands of mature trees and evidence that fine, straight timber could be grown, most of the woods would be classified as 'derelict'—abandoned coppice with trees of no timber value left after previous fellings. The oak, elm and chestnut coppice which has reached a degree of maturity tends to be very crooked which makes it almost valueless for timber. Valuations are summarised in Table C.5. The total standing volume of wood in round terms (excluding hazel coppice and shrubs such as hawthorn and elder) was estimated to be 8,706 cubic metres, that is, 141 cubic metres per hectare. The average estimated value of the standing timber etc was £541 per hectare or £3.83 per cubic metre.

Overgrown unmanaged oak and hazel coppice

Table C.5 Quantities and Values of Forest Produce

Type of produce	Species	Quantity[1] (cu m)	Standing value (£)
Sawlogs	Oak	1,069	13,804
	Ash	252	3,147
	Beech	426	4,999
	Sweet Chestnut	45	521
	Larch	946	6,861
	Scots Pine	48	275
	Norway Spruce	12	70
	Sawlog totals	2,798	29,677
Firewood		7,379 tonnes[2]	3,690
	GRAND TOTAL		£33,367

[1] Rounded to nearest whole cubic metre
[2] Green weight

C.13 **Game.** In principle, the potential for game management is considerable. The mixture of large and small woods, the variety of flight paths between them, the open meadows, the nature of the area's agriculture (with some cereal production yielding 'tail corn' for feed), the sheltered nature of the valley itself, the proximity to other (tourist) attractions which makes the development of shooting holidays possible—all would make a gound foundation for carefully planned and managed commercial shooting. Even without this speculative commercial development, the farmers could enjoy a high standard of shooting for their own pleasure. However, as Table C.2 shows, there is only a low level of interest in game, and in fact a number of farmers are actually against shooting. For these reasons, the degree of co-operation which would be needed to develop the game potential is most unlikely to be forthcoming.

Conclusion

C.14 These woods are not in any immediate danger of disappearing. They are valued for a variety of reasons by the farmers and landowners concerned, and, because of the steep ground, they are not easily reclaimable for agriculture. Over half the farmers were keenly interested in the survey and, although they tended to be against direct government intervention welcomed the idea of some 'scheme' which would add value to their woods and help make them pay their way. Nevertheless, there is still cause for concern.

C.15 First, it appears that the standard advice given by various sources recommends that broadleaved woods should be replaced by coniferous plantations as being the only crop which gives anything like a useful return on capital investment. Three of the respondents rejected this because it would change the character of their woods, but they had had no guidance on other options. Others were contemplating conversion (one had already started) in emulation of estates in other parts of the valley. If carried out on any large scale, this would certainly alter the landscape and, at the density of planting seen elsewhere, might well adversely affect the existing woodland flora.

C.16 Second, in a number of cases neglect, abuse or both is subtly affecting the character of the woods. Where old coppice is allowed to grow tall, the resulting shade tends to alter the composition of the ground flora and shrub understorey. This occurs particularly where beech and sycamore are prevalent but also under almost pure oak coppice. Because of the 'edge effect' with small woods and because the intensity of light is high, the change is not rapid, but it is probable that it will speed up unless some form of cutting cycle is resumed. Then there is the harsher effect of heavy grazing by stock both on the soil and ground flora, as well as its adverse effect (very noticeable in this study area) on natural regeneration. Oak, in particular, is a long-lived tree and there is no immediate danger of its complete destruction, but if nothing is done over three or four decades there will be steady decline and, over a century, eventual severe losses of woodland.

East Sussex

Landscape

D.1   The study area lies on the south-western edge of the Weald and was selected for its abundant woodland cover, small farm size, and because very little was known of it. It lies in the angle of a junction between the two main routes from London to Eastbourne, the A22 and the A267 (A21), with its western side formed by the minor road from Horam to Golden Cross. The other two roads in the area run roughly north to south. It lies across the gentle valley of a tributary of the Cuckmere River (see Map), seven kilometres from the South Downs Area of Outstanding Natural Beauty and eleven kilometres from the edge of Eastbourne. It is densely populated and is popular with walkers, both on and off the rights of way.

D.2   There are fairly extensive views into the valley from the major roads, giving the impression of nearby fields and distant forests. Because of the ease of viewing (and excellent road access) nearly all the woods are of landscape importance, giving, with the undulating topography, a variety of miniature landscapes.

D.3   The area covers 1,295 hectares, with 114.9 hectares of woodland, of which 9.6 hectares were cleared under felling licence in 1973 and so were not included in the survey. (Although the original licence contained a replanting condition covering the whole area, only 2.8 hectares have been replanted—with a mixture of conifers and hardwoods—and the remainder has been turned into pasture.) Houses and their gardens occupy approximately 25 hectares on the southern margin, and the remainder is farmland. It proved impossible to make contact with all of the thirty-four farmers or landowners in the area. There was evidence that some of the houses and smallholdings in the area were used as second homes. Twenty farmers or landowners with woodlands were approached. Only one refused information. Table D.1 shows the pattern of size and ownership—mainly small farms but with one large estate of five farms.

Table D.1   Size and Ownership of Farms in the East Sussex Study Area

	20 ha & below	21–40 ha	41–60 ha	61–80 ha	81–100 ha	Over 100 ha
Number of farms	5	5	2	3	—	4
Proportion of total	26%	26%	11%	16%	—	21%

(Base 19)
(Owner occupiers[1]   16)
(Tenants[1]   2)
(Information refused 1)
(Interview refused   1)
(No contact[2]   14)

[1]Farmers may both own and rent land in the area
[2]From the aerial photographs, only five had woods on their farms

D.4   The geology is simple, with Weald clay to the south, Lower Greensand and Grinstead clay to the north—giving rather acid sandy soils over clays—with evidence of impeded drainage in most of the woods and some of the lower fields. The pattern of farming is very mixed, with dairying, beef and sheep rearing, some cereals, vegetables and two stud farms. The fields are fairly small and hedged (although some hedgerows have been removed). The land is mostly good Class 3.

The Farmers

D.5   The attitudes of the farmers, owners and farm managers are also mixed, as Table D.2 shows. Apart from the game aspect, which interests few, most are mainly sympathetic to woods and wildlife, but there is also a significant minority with antagonistic views. Two farmers intend to remove their woods for agriculture, and because they "harbour vermin" (in one case, badgers), five other farmers have reclaimed woods in the last ten to fifteen years and two others have already cleared some woodland for agriculture. There is considerable interest in the financial side of land management—more so than in other study areas. The impression is that this was due to an awareness of the soaring price of land (reported to have risen from £3,700 per hectare to £5,000 in the previous year). Since the price of land under woods has remained at about £750 per hectare, there could be considerable profit to be made by clearing the woods, and there were several rumours of 'asset stripping' in the area—land being bought, its timber cleared, and then the farmhouse and land resold separately for a high profit.

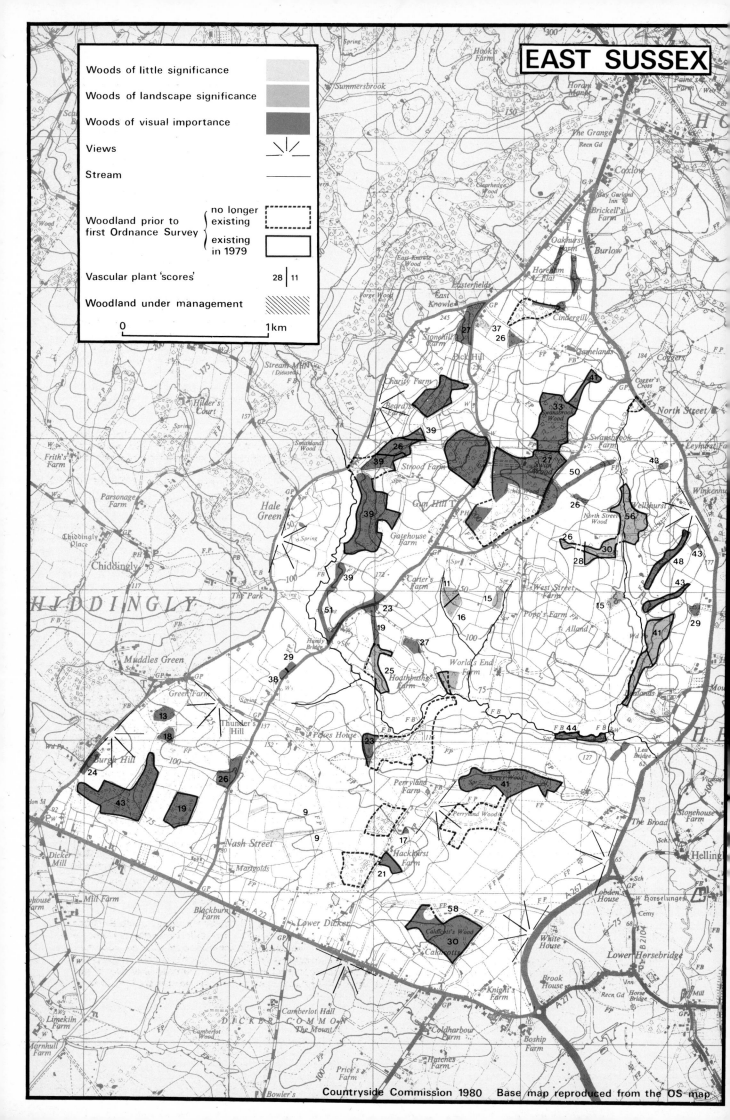

Table D.2 Attitudes to Woods in the East Sussex Study Area

	Woods/trees in general	Landscape	Wildlife	Game	Financial gain/loss
Strongly interested/ appreciative/anxious	5	2	1	1	3
Quite interested/ appreciative/anxious	4	9	8	3	6
Mildly interested/ appreciative/anxious	6	2	2	2	3
Indifferent	—	1	2	5	3
Antipathetic	2	3	4	6	2

D.6   The use made of woodlands varies. In some instances they are used for grazing cattle; one is used a paddock for horses; others are used for firewood cutting, game shooting or simple amenity. Seven farmers wanted advice on how to bring their woods under management—quite detailed advice in one case. One farmer wanted advice on how to clear his woodland altogether. Four farmers felt that their woods "should pay their way", but of these, three wished to "keep the present character" of their woods.

The Woods

D.7   The woods are distributed widely over the area (as shown on the Map), with no particular pattern except a rather higher incidence on the clay soils. There are 40 blocks of woodland which in terms of ownership and stand type differences were divided into 53 separate units: one farm with 13 woodland units; one with 6; one with 4; five with 3; four with 2; and seven with 1 wood each (one of these was being managed and was therefore excluded from the survey). From the visual evidence— especially the highly irregular edges, the list of species found, and the history of the area [23]—these woods are relicts of the ancient Wealden forest. Many are on wet areas, or on the sites of old sand quarries.

Table D.3 Areas of Woods Surveyed in the East Sussex Study Area

	Number of woods	Proportion of total (Base 52)
Less than 0.25 ha	6	11%
0.26 ha to 1 ha	21	40%
1.01 ha to 5 ha	19	36%
5.01 ha to 9.9 ha	4	8%
10 ha and over	2	4%

D.8   From the old series Ordnance Survey maps, woodland cover was more extensive in the last century (see Map). There were perhaps 156 hectares of woodland then, indicating a clearance of about 26 per cent since then. However, one farmer had paintings of the area in the 1880s which showed *less* woodland than now—possibly due to artistic licence but possibly also because some woods were managed as coppice and were probably lower on the skyline. From a management point of view the woodland in this area is of considerable interest, being largely oak standards over hornbeam coppice, some of which is still in good condition. Other woods are almost pure hornbeam coppice (becoming overgrown) together with some oak standards over chestnut coppice (also overgrown) and some good high forest.

D.9   The traditional markets were for building and joinery (for example oak standards), with the coppice and overwood going for charcoal and fuel for the Wealden iron industry, or other uses. The

Useful hornbeam coppice needing management

greensand is of moulding quality and consequently there are numerous old sand quarries in the woods. Because of the relative wealth of forest remaining in the Weald, it still has a concentration of timber industries with saw-mills, turnery works, fencing material contractors, charcoal burners and firewood merchants. A significant number of coppice craftsmen still exist, associated mainly with the chestnut coppice areas further east of the study area. There are also markets for bulk hardwoods for pulp and boards, and the demand for standing wood produce is high. All the processors spoken to reported worrying shortages of raw material supplies and the problem of fluctuations in supplies reaching the market. Access into the area is good, with some constraints due to soil conditions and to field crops (less troublesome to the charcoal burners, who prefer to burn *in situ,* using portable kilns and so removing only light loads). Some fall-off in the number of harvesting contractors was reported; and as old men retire, their places are hard to fill.

D.10   Growth in the area is good, particularly oak, ash, sweet chestnut (on the greensands) and hornbeam. Conifers do not appear to be suited to the soil or the moisture conditions—both young and older larches and pines were found to be outgrown by native species (for example the young plantation of oak with a Scots pine and Corsican pine nurse referred to in D.3 above was invisible under a dense cover of self-sown birch). However, much of the coppice is overgrown and will shortly reach an age where it will no longer re-shoot after cutting, and much is becoming derelict. In virtually every well-stocked wood the shade is too dense to permit either natural regeneration or a reasonable ground flora.

Table D.4   Types of Woodland in the East Sussex Study Area

		Number	*Proportion*
A.	Recently planted woodlands	1	2%
B.	Scrub woodland invasion	—	—
C.	Secondary regrowth on areas clearfelled 30 to 40 years ago	—	—
D.	Self-sown woods of mixed age trees and shrubs	—	—
E.	Coppice wood with few and poor standards	22	41%
F.	Overgrown coppice with standards and 'stores'	24	45%
G.	Woods and parks of mature trees with no natural regeneration	2	4%
H.	Areas recently clearfelled but no new planting	—	—
I.	Mature/semi-mature plantations (may have admixture of natural regeneration and coppice)	—	—
J.	High forest of native spp. (may have a few planted exotics)	1	2%
K.	Coppice/coppice-with-standards in good condition	3	6%
			(Base 53)

D.11   **Wildlife.** The woods are almost classic examples of acid pedunculate oak-ash-hazel or pedunculate oak-hornbeam woods, with some acid birch and alder woods. The larger and older woods, as expected, are of the highest value and yielded the highest plant scores. There is ample evidence of badgers and rabbits. There is no correlation between woodland type and plant scores but, again, grazed woods have a poorer ground flora.

D.12   **Forestry and Timber.** This is undoubtedly the most satisfactory study area from a forestry point of view. Many of the woods had been managed until the post-war years and there is a rich legacy of timber and other forest produce. Furthermore, the traditional management systems of coppice and coppice-with-standards could still be followed because good markets for the produce still exist. However, many woods will have to be cut over fairly soon if their coppicing ability (of the hornbeam and chestnut particularly) is to be retained. The strong markets for almost everything standing are reflected in the valuation in Table D.5 below. In round terms the total amount of standing wood in the surveyed woodlands was 12,480 cubic metres, or 119 cubic metres per hectare. The average value of this wood was estimated to be £2,538 per hectare or £21.41 per cubic metre.

Table D.5   Quantities and Values of Forest Produce

Type of produce	*Species*	*Quantity*[1] *(cu m)*	*Standing value (£)*
Sawlogs	Oak	4,717	228,327
	Ash	240	9,052
	Sycamore	148	2,071
	Hornbeam	92	2,222
	Beech	5	72
	Sweet Chestnut	107	1,572
	Birch	25	68
	Alder	78	214
	Larch	10	245
	Scots Pine	66	1,658
	Sawlog totals	5,488	245,501
Firewood		3,042 tonnes[2]	3,042
Charcoal		92 hectares	18,677
		GRAND TOTAL	£267,220

[1]Rounded to nearest whole cubic metre
[2]Green weight

D.13   **Game.** The game consultant was surprised at the lack of interest in shooting since the war, especially when compared with similar areas not far away and the evidence that a good deal of game management had occurred in the past. There is considerable potential for developing shooting in the area with its mild climate, thick woods, numerous boggy areas and ponds, and, of course, its proximity to London. Wild pheasant, partridge, duck, hare, rabbit, fallow deer and roe deer are all present. However, with the exception of one estate, this potential will not be realised for social reasons. First, the owners are basically not interested in game, which precludes aggregating farms into shoots. Second, the general attitude of a number of owners towards their woods is somewhat apathetic—"no management is good management"—and so the game value of their woods deteriorates. Third, the considerable use made of the area by walkers, including widespread and long established trespass, makes it difficult to manage game effectively.

Conclusion

D.14   There is something of a paradox in that the woods in this study area are in perhaps the best condition of any of the nine areas examined, and yet are probably in the most danger of deteriorating or being cleared. For social and economic reasons the land is subject to strong pressures, reflected in the very high land prices. These make it 'economic' to clear woodland for agricultural use, whether or not it is basically suitable for the purpose. Local authorities and other relevant bodies apparently find this process very difficult to resist.

D.15   Even where owners wish to retain their woodlands and resist the pressure to clear them, their very attitude in wanting to keep them static, unchanged and unexploited is leading to a breakdown in the traditional management methods which is now just on the point of becoming serious; and there is a further paradox in that the local timber processors are almost desperate for the produce of woods such as these. One processor imports three-quarters of his produce from the Continent, and has difficulty in finding enough local raw material to keep his skilled men employed. Another ranges up as far as Scotland to keep his production steady.

D16   There is also evidence of damage due to grazing, especially horses, which seem to have developed a taste for bark as well as leaves and ground vegetation. Overall, there is cause for concern for the continued existence of some woods. Insofar as the facts can be established, some 40 per cent of the losses mentioned in D.8 took place in the post-war years, and more woodland clearance is already planned. Timber and wildlife values will very soon begin to deteriorate unless these woods can be brought back under management.

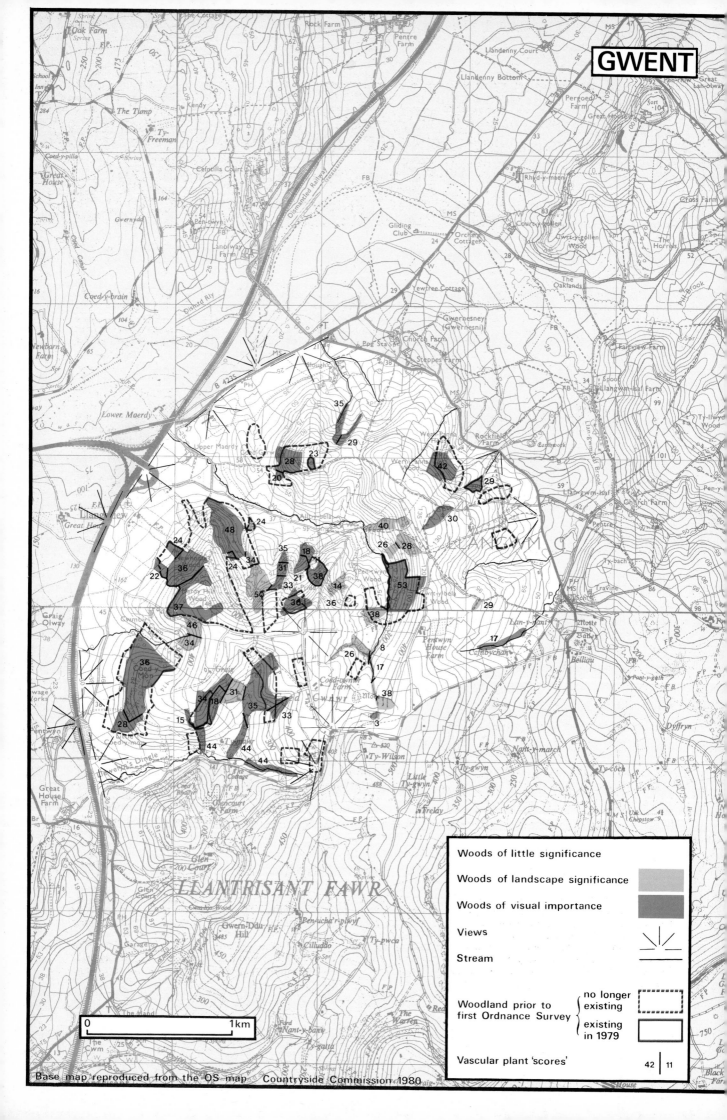

GWENT

Woods of little significance		
Woods of landscape significance		
Woods of visual importance		
Views		
Stream		
Woodland prior to first Ordnance Survey	no longer existing	
	existing in 1979	
Vascular plant 'scores'		42 | 11

Base map reproduced from the OS map   Countryside Commission 1980

Gwent

Landscape

E.1   This study area was the first to be chosen and was the location for the pilot study. The simplest description is one of a deeply dissected low plateau which itself is the outlier of the sandstone hills rising to the Wentwood Ridge. It is bordered by the A449 (Newport to Monmouth) dual carriageway, a trunk route which links the South Wales M4 with the Midlands via the M50. The other boundaries are the B4235 (Chepstow to Usk) road to the north and east, and a minor road to the south. There are also several green lanes and footpaths. The centre of the area is served by one minor road on the western side, with two others leaving it to run eastwards. Usk is just over two kilometres away; Newport and Cardiff are fourteen kilometres and thirty kilometres away respectively. There are no settlements in the area itself (see Map).

E.2   There is a steep scarp to the west, forming the skyline to travellers on the A449, with broken country behind it. The area is drained by a number of streams which occupy deeply cut valleys, and views may be had along one of these from the main road and from the lane which follows it. The area has its share of those motorists, horse-riders and walkers who appreciate its quiet beauty, but most pass along its margins and do not see the hidden country above. Consequently the most visually important woods are along the slope of the western scarp, with a number carrying Tree Preservation Orders. With its numerous woods, hedges and trees and small fields, the area is typical of much of the countryside in the Welsh Marches.

E.3   It is also the smallest area studied. Its 654 hectares include 86.9 hectares of woodland, of which 83 are unmanaged. The remainder is agricultural. The size and ownership pattern of the farms is given in Table E.1 which shows it to be predominantly an area of small, owner-occupied farms but with a complexity of rented and shared land and land in family trust.

Table E.1   Size and Ownership of Farms in the Gwent Study Area

	20 ha & below	21–40 ha	41–60 ha	61–80 ha	81–100 ha	Over 100 ha
Number of farms	2	8	1	4	3	1
Proportion of total	11%	42%	5%	21%	16%	5%

(Base 19)
(Owner-occupiers[1]   14)
(Tenants/Trust[1]   6)
(Refusals   —)
(No contact   3)

[1]Farmers may both own and rent land in the area

E.4   The hills which form the study area are of Devonian Lower Red Sandstone and, to the extreme north-east of the area, Silurian limestone. Along the Usk valley are narrow strips of alluvium and river gravels. The soils are reddish, neutral clay-loams which, coupled with the topographical constraints, give rise to lower Class 3 (and some Class 4) agricultural land. The main agricultural enterprises are livestock and dairying but with some arable, mainly for forage. This area comes closest of all those studied to a hill-farming pattern of occupancy and agriculture, with mainly traditional methods and relatively slow land-scape change.

The Farmers

E.5   Nineteen farmers were approached and none refused an interview. Over two-thirds have cleared some woodland since taking over their present land, and three plan to continue reclaiming woods for pasture. Much of the clearance appears to have been to remove scrub invasion but more substantial clearance has taken place on three farms, with perhaps 26 hectares having been reclaimed. One farmer with a Tree Preservation Order on one wood is deliberately grazing it heavily in order to destroy it. Another had carried out extensive new planting in two woods, which were consequently excluded from the survey. Three were too reticent for their underlying attitudes to be gauged, and they were therefore excluded from the summaries in Table E.2. Those interviewed were, in general, sympathetic to woods, wildlife and the landscape, but their woods do not reflect this attitude.

Table E.2 Attitudes to Woods in the Gwent Study Area

	Woods/trees in general	Landscape	Wildlife	Game	Financial gain/loss
Strongly interested/ appreciative/anxious	6	4	5	—	4
Quite interested/ appreciative/anxious	4	6	3	2	3
Mildly interested/ appreciative/anxious	5	3	4	6	4
Indifferent	—	2	3	7	4
Antipathetic	1	1	1	1	—
Inapplicable	—	—	—	—	1

E.6 Twelve farmers requested a second interview and showed a lively interest in the tenative valuations made and in the possibility of grants (although one was against grants because of the way they were "hedged round with conditions"). Sources of advice and information were requested, and advice was also sought on markets for wood produce and on contractors: three farmers had had unsatisfactory experiences with contractors.

The Woods

E.7 The distribution of the woods is shown on the Map. They occupy mainly the steeper slopes and the sides of streams and dingles. Smaller woods are located in old quarries, around springs and on hilltops. There are approximately eighteen blocks of continuous woodland which, divided by ownership and by stand type for survey purposes, comprise 53 smaller woodland units. Of these, one farm has 10 woods; one has 6; two have 4; five have 3; four have 2; and six have 1 wood. The areas of unmanaged woods are shown in Table E.3.

Table E.3 Areas of Woods Surveyed in the Gwent Study Area

	Number of woods	Proportion of total (Base 51)
Less than 0.25 ha[1]	—	—
0.26 ha to 1 ha	27	53%
1.01 ha to 5 ha	22	43%
5.01 to 9.9 ha	2	4%
10 ha and over	—	—

[1] Woods of this size were not surveyed in the pilot study

E.8 From the old series Ordnance Survey maps, it appears that the area under woodland has been reduced by about 17 per cent, which is approximately the area claimed to have been cleared by the present farmers. However, the cleared areas do not coincide with the woodland boundary changes shown on the Map. One farm in the area, whose ownership is disputed, has had no occupant for some ten years, and is fast being invaded by birch and alder scrub. It is quite probable that the long agricultural depression in the 1890s may well have resulted in an increase in wooded areas, with periodic reclamation in times of agricultural prosperity. (It is also noticeable that some of the woodland 'cleared' by farmers is regrowing). What is clear is that some woods were formerly much bigger.

E.9 Traditionally, woodland management in the area appears to have tended towards coppice-with-standards: the standards going for sawlogs, the larger coppice (oak and ash) for pit props (hardwood props were traditionally used in the Forest of Dean coal mines until the 1960s), and the smaller coppice (hazel) for the usual estate and farm purposes, such as sheep hurdles. That many of the woods were managed in the past is evident from the extensive introduction of beech. The present day markets are for sawlogs, turnery poles, mining chocks, pulpwood and branches for racing hurdles. The demand is (subject to season) high, with the South Wales coalfields to the west and the Forest of Dean saw-mills and other wood industries to the east. There is a hardwood pulp mill only fifteen kilometres away, and the industrial Midlands are within easy reach. However, access is often difficult because of the terrain, the narrow lanes and the clay soils. There also appears to be a shortage of good contractors able and willing to work small woodlands.

E.10 Growth rates are good. One wood whose last felling year is known suggests a growth rate, under proper management, of 12 cubic metres per hectare per year, with birch and several other species showing healthy growth. The character of the woods is indicated by Table E.4.

Table E.4 Types of Woodland in the Gwent Study Area

		Number	Proportion
A.	Recently planted woodlands	2	4%
B.	Scrub woodland invasion	1	2%
C.	Secondary regrowth on areas clearfelled 30 to 40 years ago	3	6%
D.	Self-sown woods of mixed age trees and shrubs	9	17%
E.	Coppice wood with few and poor standards	9	17%
F.	Overgrown coppice with standards and 'stores'	13	24%
G.	Woods and parks of mature trees with no natural regeneration	9	17%
H.	Areas recently clearfelled but no new planting	7	13%
I.	Mature/semi-mature plantations (may have admixture of natural regeneration and coppice)	—	—
J.	High forest of native spp. (may have a few planted exotics)	—	—
K.	Coppice/coppice-with-standards in good condition	—	—

(Base 53)

E.11 **Wildlife.** Using the Nature Conservancy Council's Stand Type classifications [62], the woods may be intermediate between wet ash-maple and acid pedunculate oak-ash-hazel, together with alderwoods on the wet areas (particularly along and under a spring line on the lower scarp slopes). Some have a very high wildlife value as measured by the vascular plant scores, being associated both with 'old' woods and newer ones. It seems probable from the botanical evidence that some woods with high scores are probably relict woods and were missed by the original surveyor. However, heavy grazing is altering the character of many woods, and the closure of canopy on much of the overgrown coppice is having adverse effects on ground flora.

E.12 **Forestry and Timber.** Although plundered for their timber in the past, especially during two World Wars and in the 1930's when the old estates were broken up, there are a number of reasonably useful woods with good oak, ash, cherry and aspen just reaching maturity. However, stocking is light except in the larger woods and a good deal of crown thinning is needed in the now overgrown coppice woods. Because of the range of markets in the area, a number of silvicultural options are open to the forester, including twelve to fourteen year pulpwood rotations of coppice, and birch and alder regeneration (if the woods can be fenced). The practice of using many woods for sheltering livestock and grazing is beginning to have visible effects on stocking, particularly near the edges where deterioration towards a park-like condition of isolated trees in grass is evident. The total standing volume of wood in round terms was estimated at 5,760 cubic metres, or 69 cubic metres per hectare. The values in round terms placed on the possible produce are summarised in Table E.5—the average being £551 per hectare or £7.95 per cubic metre.

Moribund coppice with standards

Table E.5 Quantities and Values of Forest Produce

Type of produce	Species	Quantity[1] (cu m)	Standing value (£)
Sawlogs	Oak	649	12,964
	Ash	1,223	20,215
	Beech	59	312
	Elm	40	221
	Birch	32	178
	Cherry	173	7,199
	Larch	12	234
	Sawlog totals	2,188	41,323
Pulpwood		3,141 tonnes[2]	3,141
Firewood		2,636 tonnes[2]	1,318
		GRAND TOTAL	£45,782

[1]Rounded to nearest whole cubic metre
[2]Green weight

E.13   **Game.** There is no tradition of managed shooting in this part of Gwent, and the farmers interviewed have no great interest in rough shooting either. Neglect and mismanagement have also reduced their game value. The steep, often north-facing slopes and the wind-funnelling valleys mean that thick-edged, warm woods are needed to induce game to stay. There is little arable land, and cover crops are scarce. Therefore, at present, the potential for game management is low. In principle, the area as a whole could sustain a game enterprise with a full-time gamekeeper, etc, but the high costs involved and the unwillingness to co-operate which was clear from the interviews, suggest little scope for improvement.

Conclusion

E.14   Many of the woodlands in the area are in the process of disappearing, through deliberate action or neglect. The speed at which this will happen will depend on the species mix in each wood but, given the high proportion of relatively short-lived (under present management) species such as birch, alder, aspen and willow, it could be rapid. Conversely, there is a problem due to neglected woods becoming overgrown, with consequent wind damage or adverse shading effects on ground vegetation. This is due in part to financial pressures but is more directly attributable to a lack of knowledge and to a general level of apathy which co-exist with the declared sympathy felt by farmers for their woods. Yet there is an opportunity to bring about a change: on one hand many woods need thinning or even clearcutting (coppice); on the other there are markets close at hand eager for forest produce. What is missing is a source of unbiased advice and supervision, and some means of connecting these woodland resources with the markets.

Lincolnshire

Landscape

F.1 The area lies wholly within the Lincolnshire Wolds Area of Outstanding Natural Beauty, between the chalk scarp and the flat fenland. It is a gently undulating area with wide panoramic views and a central ridge which divides it into two visual entities. There are no major roads in or bounding the area, but it lies near the base of a triangle formed by the A158 (Lincoln to Skegness), the A16 (Boston to Grimsby), and the A153 (Horncastle to Louth). The boundaries chosen run along the Bluestone Heath road to the north, with rather *ad hoc* boundaries drawn along roads, footpaths and estate boundaries on the other sides.

F.2 There is a complex pattern of county and private roads joining farms and the seven villages in the area. They frequently follow ridges, and, as they are often hedgeless and fenceless, offer many good viewpoints into the area. All parts of the area are visible from at least one of these roads. From the Bluestone Heath road there are panoramic views across the area to the valley of the River Bain and the Fens beyond. Horncastle is five kilometres away, Skegness twenty, and Lincoln forty. Because of this openness, the woods are almost all visually important, except perhaps a dozen or so which are set low and are not visible from roads. Hedgerows, where they still exist, are trimmed to a low height and several new hedges have recently been planted. There are a number of footpaths, and the 'Viking Way' footpath runs through the area.

F.3 The surface area is 4,615 hectares, of which about 48 hectares may be regarded as 'built-up'. Of the 114.5 hectares of woodland, 14.8 hectares are being managed and so were not surveyed; the remainder is agricultural land, with large holdings, as Table F.1 shows.

Table F.1   Size and Ownership of Farms in the Lincolnshire Study Area

	20 ha & below	21–40 ha	41–60 ha	61–80 ha	81–100 ha	Over 100 ha
Number of farms	2	2	1	3	2	15
Proportion of total (Base 25)	8%	8%	4%	12%	8%	60%

(Owner-occupiers[1]   18)
(Tenants[1]   7)
(Refusals   2)
(No contact   1)

[1]Farmers may both own and rent land in the area

F.4 The geology is of Red Chalk on the scarp to the north, and Spilsby Sandstone on the long slopes below, with Kimmeridge Clay underlying both at the surface in the south, and overlying Boulder Clays to the west. The soils are mostly light and porous, but require careful management for cereal production which is the major land use on the Class 2 and good Class 3 soils. However, a variety of other crops are grown: sugar beet, potatoes and other roots. Grass leys needed to maintain good soil structure carry a good deal of livestock, including sheep. Intensive pig and poultry units are also found. Altogether it is a gentle, fertile, prosperous-looking farming area.

The Farmers

F.5 There are twenty-seven farmers in the area, seven of whom have no woods on their land. Two farmers refused a first interview, but eight of those with woodland asked for a second interview. One estate is beginning to bring its woods under management—mainly by clearfelling and replanting (again with conifers, conifer and hardwood mixtures, and hybrid poplar) mixed, with fairly positive attitudes towards trees and woods but in three instances with the proviso that "they should be in management". One farmer intends to plant trees in about two years' time. The attitudes of the farmers and farm managers are mixed, with fairly positive attitudes towards trees and woods but, in three instances with the proviso that "they should be in their place". One farmer said he would "pull up the lot of them" if he had his way. Attitudes to financial aspects (including grants) are very negative, whilst those towards game are totally the opposite. The attitude to the wildlife value of woods is mainly one of indifference, and, to landscape, somewhat mixed.

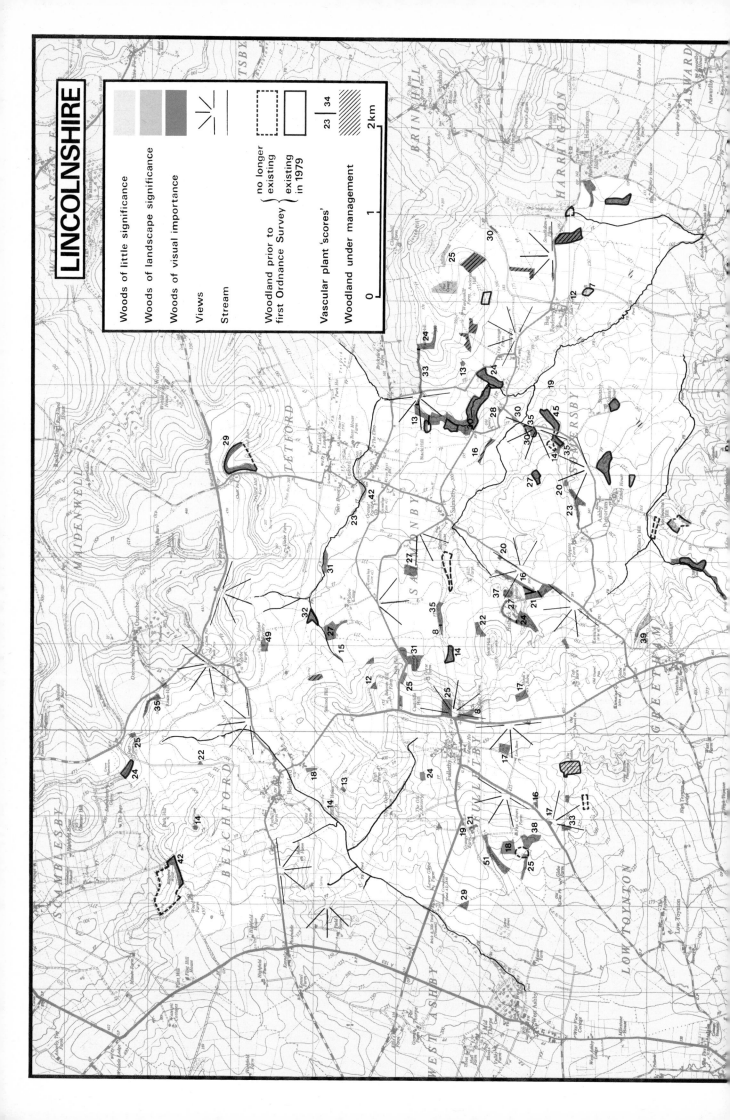

LINCOLNSHIRE

Woods of little significance

Woods of landscape significance

Woods of visual importance

Views

Stream

Woodland prior to first Ordnance Survey { no longer existing / existing in 1979 }

Vascular plant 'scores'   23 | 34

Woodland under management

0   1   2km

Table F.2 Attitudes to Woods in the Lincolnshire Study Area

	Woods/trees in general	Landscape	Wildlife	Game	Financial gain/loss
Strongly interested/ appreciative/anxious	4	5	4	8	—
Quite interested/ appreciative/anxious	12	6	3	4	2
Mildly interested/ appreciative/anxious	2	2	1	3	2
Indifferent	—	5	10	1	10
Antipathetic	2	1	1	2	3
Inapplicable	—	1	1	2	3

F.6   At the second interviews advice on woodland management was requested by one farmer who was interested to hear of the availability of grants, and it emerged that two others had already received assistance. In general, in both sets of interviews it became clear that there is an awareness of grant aid and advice, but woods and trees are lower in priority than agriculture.

The Woods

F.7   The distribution of the woods is shown on the Map. They lie in rounded clumps on hill and ridge tops; in thin belts just below the chalk scarp; in what were probably plantations around the manor and farm houses; and along boggy patches and small streams along the spring line. There are 102 woods, 20 of which are being managed. One estate with three tenant farms in the area has 33 woods which are kept 'in hand', of which 11 are managed. Of the other farms surveyed, one has 11 woods; two have 9 (including 2 managed); one has 8 (with 2 managed); one has 6 (with 1 managed); three have 4; one has 3; three have 2; and four have 1 wood (with 1 managed).

Table F.3 Areas of Woods Surveyed in the Lincolnshire Study Area

	Number of woods	Proportion of total (Base 82)
Less than 0.25 ha	25	30%
0.26 ha to 1 ha	23	28%
1.01 ha to 5 ha	32	39%
5.01 ha to 9.9 ha	1	1%
10 ha and over	1	1%

F.8   From a comparison with the old series Ordnance Survey maps, it is apparent that the area of woodland and the number of individual woods have actually increased by approximately 46 per cent since the maps were first published. From the plant counts, some of the woods are probably relicts of the 'wildwood' [60]. Many of the apparently newer woods were probably planted for game. Ash and elm are rather more in evidence (and have generally grown better) than oak, and the virulent strain of Dutch elm disease has not yet reached the area, although the disease itself is present. From the evidence, the traditional management appears to have been a form of coppice-with-standards, with newer woods tending to be high forest. Good markets were reported for sawlogs of most species in the area. There is one hardwood saw-mill in Horncastle itself and others which, whilst they are at some distance, have a wide catchment for logs. On the other hand, the markets for smallwood are poor. Access is excellent, with a good road system and all-weather farm roads for the highly mechanised farming of the area. There are an adequate number of contractors in the region as a whole.

Isolated copse of great landscape value

F.9   Growth conditions vary widely, being relatively poor on the chalk (where only sycamore and beech have done well) and fair to good elsewhere. Alder grows particularly well along the spring line. There are the remains of conifer planting in many woods but these do not seem happy, with European larch and Scots pine faring best and the Norway spruce doing badly. Elm and larch logs from the same wood were almost identical in length and butt size. What is striking is the lack of regeneration either from coppice or from seedlings. Most of the woods are not grazed, yet open spaces covered in bracken and nettles are well developed in quite a number. Where felling has taken place, only hawthorn and elder appear to have regenerated; the Nature Conservancy Council suggest this is because of rabbits and hares. The net result is a slow reduction in the number of trees and a transformation from rather derelict high forest to scrub with a scatter of old trees. For game purposes, some edge planting of mainly evergreen species has been carried out apparently to counteract this tendency.

Table F.4 Types of Woodland in the Lincolnshire Study Area

		Number	Proportion
A.	Recently planted woodlands	20	20%
B.	Scrub woodland invasion	5	5%
C.	Secondary regrowth on areas clearfelled 30 to 40 years ago	3	3%
D.	Self-sown woods of mixed age trees and shrubs	17	17%
E.	Coppice wood with few and poor standards	4	4%
F.	Overgrown coppice with standards and 'stores'	19	19%
G.	Woods and parks of mature trees with no natural regeneration	22	21%
H.	Areas recently clearfelled but no new planting	3	3%
I.	Mature/semi-mature plantations (may have admixture of natural regeneration and coppice)	9	9%
J.	High forest of native spp. (may have a few planted exotics)	—	—
K.	Coppice/coppice-with-standards in good condition	—	—
			(Base 102)

F.10 **Wildlife.** Where classification was possible, the woods appeared to be a mixture of the suckering elm, maple and acid birch oak stand types, with almost pure alder along the flushes. A number of woods have a high wildlife value and although some of them are not on the old series Ordnance Survey maps, the botanical evidence suggests that they are of considerable age: a similar observation was made in the Gwent area. There is no correlation apparent with the woodland types detailed in Table F.4. Two of the woods contain Sites of Special Scientific Interest.

F.11 **Forestry and Timber.** Such management as there is appears mainly game-orientated. There are no really good stands of timber and, as noted above, virtually no natural regeneration, so tree stock levels are poor. Potentially valuable windblown trees such as cherry are left to rot. Standards are poor in form, and oak (usually the most valuable timber) is extremely prone to small epicormic knotting. Ash and elm however are of good form and growth. Some of the recently established mixed plantations need urgent crown thinning to give the beech a chance. Planting in others is widely spaced, presumably for game sightlines. Table F.5 shows the outcome of the valuations made for the woods. The total standing volume of wood in the unmanaged woods was about 10,778 cubic metres, or 108 cubic metres per hectare. The estimated average value of the standing timber and other produce was £638 per hectare or £5.90 per cubic metre.

Table F.5 Quantities and Values of Forest Produce

Type of produce	Species	Quantity[1] (cu m)	Standing value (£)
Sawlogs	Oak	182	4,699
	Ash	891	23,199
	Beech	375	3,566
	Sycamore	677	8,766
	Elm	1,419	15,210
	Alder	190	569
	Poplar	66	526
	Lime	10	112
	Cherry	3	228
	Yew	1	250
	Larch	102	1,146
	Other conifers	65	731
	Sawlog totals	3,981	59,002
Firewood		9,158 tonnes[2]	4,576
	GRAND TOTAL		£63,578

[1] Rounded to nearest whole cubic metre
[2] Green weight

F.12 **Game.** The area has a long tradition of sporting interest, being predominantly a pheasant shooting area but with a still considerable amount of partridge shooting. On the larger estates many activities are subordinated to game interests—a fact not without significance for the state of the woods. Woodlands occupy a small percentage of the area and, because of this and because of the removal of hedgerows, they represent a very large proportion of the available cover and roosting places. Some of the planting carried out to improve the game-holding capacity of woods has not been well done, for example Norway spruce is definitely not a suitable species for most sites in the area but has been much used. Much remains to be done to windproof woods already used for rearing birds. Given the interest in shooting, there is some potential for further development especially if the present small neighbouring shoots combine their resources. And in purely commercial terms, accommodation is available in the area which could make shooting holidays a viable proposition, the income from which could offset the costs of improvement. The agriculture of the area is also well suited to game management, but considerable improvement to the woods is needed to realise the full potential.

Conclusion

F.13 As there is a considerable amount of goodwill towards woods in the area, and as they are highly valued for game, there is very little danger of them being removed for other land uses. However, their condition and the lack of regeneration appears to be leading to a slow decline which is already visible at some distance. This change will be exacerbated when the more virulent strain of Dutch elm disease reaches the area, since elm is such an important component of many of the woods.

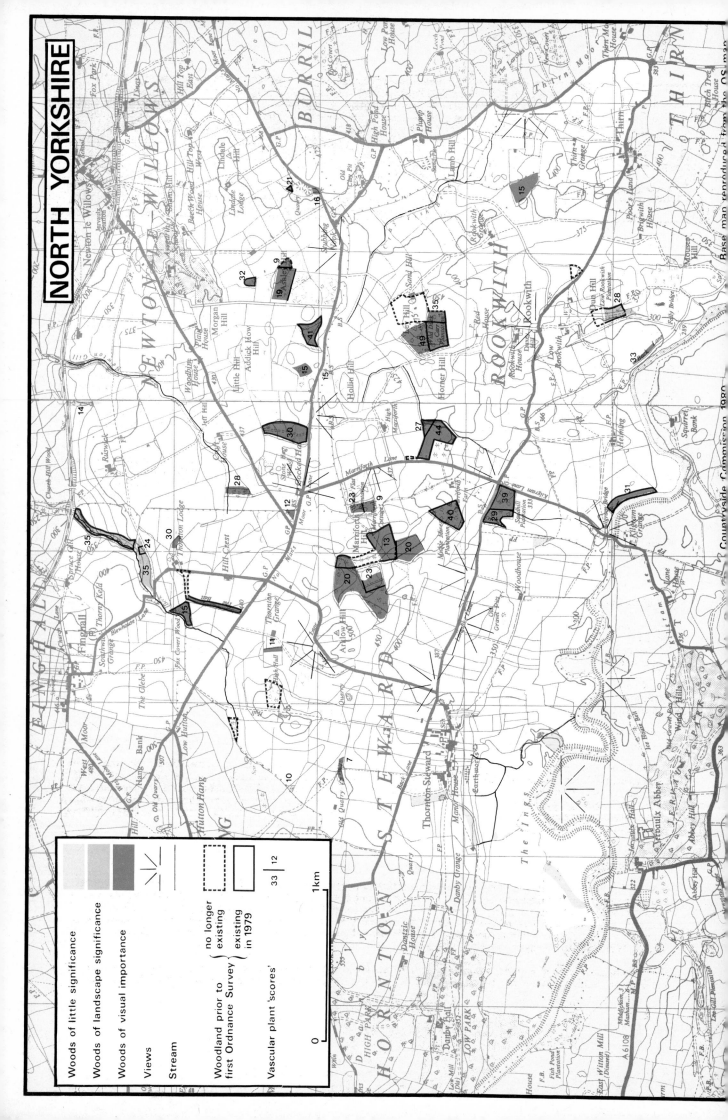

NORTH YORKSHIRE

Legend:

Woods of little significance

Woods of landscape significance

Woods of visual importance

Views

Stream

Woodland prior to first Ordnance Survey
- no longer existing
- existing in 1979

33 | 12 Vascular plant 'scores'

0   1km

North Yorkshire

Landscape

G.1   The study area is located on the eastern edge of Wensleydale—its eastern boundary being just over five kilometres from the Yorkshire Dales National Park—in the angle between the A684 (Northallerton to Kendal) and the A6108 (Ripon to Richmond) roads. At its closest, the A1 passes just over seven kilometres away. Masham and Bedale are each seven kilometres away, Ripon and York sixteen and fifty-six respectively. The area lies across a shallow ridge between the River Ure and Bedale Beck. The Map shows the nature of the area.

G.2   The final boundaries were selected as the Northallerton to Leyburn Railway to the north, the River Ure to the south, and minor roads and footpaths to the east and west. The area is well served by minor roads, and contains one village and three hamlets. The topography has the typical rolling appearance of a former outwash plain and is an important element in the panoramic views obtained from the A6108 and Wilton Fell across the river. There is also an excellent view of the area from the river bridge near Jervaulx Abbey. Within the area the hedges are trimmed low, and a number of smaller-scale landscapes are revealed from its internal roads, particularly from those travelling east to west. It is a pleasant, well-groomed, open landscape with both large and small fields, with woods being extremely important landscape elements.

G.3   The study area covers about 1,351 hectares. There are 78.5 hectares of woodland, of which 13.3 are being managed and so were not surveyed. Settlements cover 16.1 hectares, and another 12.5 hectares are taken up by a park surrounding a public school. The remainder is agricultural land. It contains twenty-one farms, and interviews were obtained at fifteen of them. The pattern of farm size and ownership given in Table G.1 is characterised by owner-occupation on mainly 60- to 100-hectare holdings.

Table G.1   Size and Ownership of Farms in the North Yorkshire Study Area

	20 ha & below	21–40 ha	41–60 ha	61–80 ha	81–100 ha	Over 100 ha
Number of farms	2	1	1	4	6	1
Proportion of total (Base 15)	13%	7%	7%	27%	40%	7%

(Owner occupiers[1]   15)
(Tenants[1]   1)
(Not interviewed because
    had no woods   2)
(Refusals   —)
(No contact   3)

[1]Farmers may both own and rent land in the area

G.4   The geology consists of Magnesian Limestone to the north-east and Millstone Grit across the remainder. However, there are deep drifts of glacial sands and gravels to the east and Boulder Clay across the western side, with some alluvium in the south. The soils are mostly deep and well-drained good Class 3 agricultural land. The agriculture is mainly beef and sheep with some dairying and cereal growing. Hedges appear to have been retained (with some replanting) and are well trimmed. Farm buildings are a mixture of old and modern giving the overall impression of a modern intensively farmed area which still uses traditional methods to a substantial degree.

The Farmers

G.5   Of the fifteen farmers who were interviewed ten asked for a second interview out of general interest and to seek further management advice. One farmer has reclaimed 2.5 hectares of woodland for agriculture, but has also selectively felled to favour ash and oak saplings in other woods. Altogether, six farmers have carried out some woodland management, mainly felling and replanting, usually with conifer and broadleaved mixtures (one having received a Forestry Commission Small Woods Grant for the purpose). Most of the woods are fenced off and uncontrolled grazing was evident on only three farms which had woods felled in World War II and again in the early 1960s.

G.6   There is a strong appreciation of woodlands in this area, and there was a keen interest in the project itself. The respondents are, in the main, highly aware of and articulate about the relevance of woods and hedges to landscape and wildlife, but they are also well aware of the financial implications. Table G.2 shows something of this pattern of interest. Advice was sought on management options and on planting grants, and also on the possible sale of standing timber.

Table G.2 Attitudes to Woods in the North Yorkshire Study Area

	Woods/trees in general	Landscape	Wildlife	Game	Financial gain/loss
Strongly interested/ appreciative/anxious	6	8	3	7	—
Quite interested/ appreciative/anxious	6	2	6	5	6
Mildly interested/ appreciative/anxious	2	4	3	1	1
Indifferent	1	1	3	2	8
Antipathetic	—	—	—	—	—

The Woods

G.7   The woods are distributed mainly along the upper part of the shallow ridge and appear to be almost entirely plantations in origin. The area was said to have been formerly a large shooting estate, and the game consultant's opinion is that their shapes and siting suggest game cover as the original objective. Accordingly they do not entirely accentuate the topography (as in most other areas) or suggest, even with linking hedgerows, any degree of homogeneity. Sub-divided by stand type, there are 47 woods in the area, of which 10 are managed. One farm has 11 woods, one farm has 5; three have 4; two have 3; four have 2; and five have 1 wood. Table G.3 shows the sizes of the woods.

Table G.3 Areas of Woods Surveyed in the North Yorkshire Study Area

	Number of woods	Proportion of total (Base 37)
Less than 0.25 ha	5	13%
0.26 ha to 1 ha	18	49%
1.01 ha to 5 ha	13	35%
5.01 ha to 9.9 ha	1	3%
10 ha and over	—	—

G.8   Since publication of the old series Ordnance Survey maps there has been a net increase in woodland cover of approximately 26 per cent. As previously noted, the woods are almost entirely of plantation origin, managed partly for timber and partly for game, but after the break-up of the old estate during the inter-war years they were largely robbed of their better timber, particularly the larch and pine and, in the older woods to the north-west, the oak standards. There is some evidence of coppice management in the past, but most woods were managed (in forestry terms) towards high forest. Their timber was probably utilised on the estate, and later on sold for general purpose saw-milling. Present markets are good for sawlogs in a range of qualities, but prices are fairly low except for better quality oak and ash. Interestingly, the demand for sycamore appears rather higher here than in most other areas studied—perhaps because its resistance to exposure gives it a greater local incidence than in milder, more southerly areas, and gives rise to a

A neglected old conifer plantation

proportionately greater amount which must be disposed of. There are at least five medium-sized hardwood sawmills within sixty kilometres. There is, however a poor market for smallwood except as firewood. Access is fairly good, with a reasonable terrain and roads close by.

G.9   Growth rates appear only fair, a measure of the shorter growing season in this, the most north-easterly study area. However, good timber can be grown. The general character of the woods is set out in Table G.4.

Table G.4 Types of Woodland in the North Yorkshire Study Area

		Number	Proportion
A.	Recently planted woodlands	10	21%
B.	Scrub woodland invasion	5	11%
C.	Secondary regrowth on areas clearfelled 30 to 40 years ago	2	4%
D.	Self-sown woods of mixed age trees and shrubs	5	11%
E.	Coppice wood with few and poor standards	8	17%
F.	Overgrown coppice with standards and 'stores'	2	4%
G.	Woods and parks of mature trees with no natural regeneration	3	6%
H.	Areas recently clearfelled but no new planting	4	8%
I.	Mature/semi-mature plantations (may have admixture of natural regeneration and coppice)	6	13%
J.	High Forest of native spp. (may have a few planted exotics)	2	4%
K.	Coppice/coppice-with-standards in good condition	—	—

(Base 47)

G.10 Wildlife. The plant scores are shown on the Map and have some relationship to the relative age of the woods. However, the differences in scores are at least partly due to the widespread use of some woods for grazing. Higher scores, as in all study areas, are also associated with wetter sites. Rabbits are abundant but little other animal life was evident during the winter survey.

G.11 Forestry and Timber. A few of the more recently planted woods are well looked after, but other plantations have not been weeded properly and have suffered losses accordingly. Although there is some regeneration in the older woods—mainly of sycamore—their general condition is somewhat moribund. This is at least partly due to the selective removal of the best stems (referred to earlier), leaving the poorer, slowly growing, more crooked trees. Some crown thinning and culling of suppressed trees is needed or, preferably, underplanting or group replanting. A small number of mainly conifer plantations are mature enough for clearfelling. The valuations placed on the woods are summarised in Table G.5. The total standing wood volume was estimated at 4,691 cubic metres, or 72 cubic metres per hectare. The average value was estimated to be £419 per hectare, or £5.83 per cubic metre.

Table G.5 Quantities and Values of Forest Produce

Type of produce	Species	Quantity[1] (cu m)	Standing value (£)
Sawlogs	Oak	132	3,840
	Ash	110	3,890
	Beech	153	1,928
	Sycamore	510	5,661
	Elm	89	368
	Alder	210	874
	Larch	282	3,868
	Scots Pine	320	4,806
	Norway Spruce	27	265
	Sawlog totals	1,833	25,500
Firewood		3,746 tonnes[2]	1,873
	GRAND TOTAL		£27,373

[1]Rounded to nearest whole cubic metre
[2]Green weight

G.12 Game. From its old status as a large sporting estate, there is a residual but widespread interest in shooting. There are also syndicated shooting estates on the borders of the area. However, little practical management has been carried out. As with most of the areas studied, the small size of holdings precludes any one farmer successfully establishing a game enterprise, but the keen interest shown could mean there is scope for a co-operative approach. As stated in G.7, the woods are well laid out for game management, but in most the age and size of the majority of trees means that, at least at the edges, thickening up by new planting is needed to give greater shelter and warmth in this fairly exposed northerly area. Pheasant and duck offer the most potential for a managed shoot, but partridge are also present in the area. The reasonably mixed nature of the farming on some of the arable land is also encouraging, with the substantial amount of cereal cropping offering a relatively inexpensive source of feed to rear birds.

Conclusion

G.13   The future of these woods seems reasonably well-assured, at least in their present state. Their plantation origins and comparative youth are contributing factors, and in that context the lack of natural regeneration is not worrying. There have already been significant replantings, competently done, and whilst they are coniferous in nature, so probably were their predecessors, so the landscape change will be minimal in the medium term. However, a number of the younger woods should now be opened up a little, perhaps with some group or underplanting. Parts of the area once grew good oak, and could do so again if the owners approached woodland management in the right way, but beech and sycamore seem to be preferred.

G.14   From a wildlife point of view, understandable though it is in an area which has its share of bleak winter conditions, the widespread practice of using woods for shelter and for grazing is having adverse effects on the quantity and range of species of ground flora.

Somerset

Landscape

H.1   The study area is situated on the north-western edge of the Vale of Taunton, roughly half-way between the Brendon Hills and the Quantocks (an Area of Outstanding Natural Beauty), its margins being approximately five kilometres and three kilometres from their respective boundaries. The A361 (Taunton to Barnstaple) runs close by—and overlooks—the area's southern boundary, whilst the A358 (Taunton to Minehead) road runs parallel to its north-eastern boundary. It is nine kilometres from Taunton. The area has an intricate network of minor roads and footpaths, some of which also form its boundaries. These minor roads are, however, mostly banked and hedged so that views from within the area are severely restricted. The northern part, beyond the dividing stream, Halse Water, is deeply dissected by small valleys, many of which have streams. The south is dominated by a steep, south-facing scarp, with a tongue of the Vale of Taunton extending into its eastern edge.

H.2   There is a considerable contrast between the north and the south; the former characterised by small farms with small fields, the latter by larger farms and fields. There are two small hamlets within the area and two more on the eastern margin. Although near major tourist routes, it is not much used by tourists, but it has within it a major food-processing plant which attracts a significant number of visitors, including holidaymakers. Because of the busy neighbouring roads and the views into the area, nearly all its woods are visually important, accentuating the undulating topography by their location on tops of hills and along scarp slopes and streams. Individual woods are frequently linked by overgrown hedgerows to form a continuous horizon of trees, thereby giving a markedly wooded character to the area in contrast to the adjacent flat and comparatively treeless Vale of Taunton.

H.3   The area covers 1,545 hectares. Woodlands cover 51.8 hectares, of which 50.2 are unmanaged. The rest, except two hectares of settlement, is under agriculture. Table H.1 shows the size and ownership patterns of farms in the area.

Table H.1 Size and Ownership of Farms in the Somerset Study Area

		20 ha & below	21–40 ha	41–60 ha	61–80 ha	81–100 ha	Over 100 ha
Number of farms		—	7	5	4	—	1
Proportion of total		—	41%	29%	24%	—	6%
(Base 17)							
(Owner-occupiers[1]	16)						
(Tenants[1]	1)						
(No information	3)						
(Refusals	3)						

[1]Farmers may both own and rent land in the area

H.4   The geology is Triassic and Permian represented by Upper and Lower Sandstones, Upper and Lower Marls, and Pebble Beds. The agricultural land is mainly Class 3. Farming is principally livestock and dairying, but with some cereal and other arable land. There is a marked contrast between the predominantly traditional farming methods in the north and the more mechanised, intensive farming in the south.

The Farmers

H.5   Of the thirty farmers in the area, seven have no woods at all, and three refused access and interviews. Of the remaining twenty farmers with woods three were too busy to be interviewed, but allowed access to their woods. Two farmers have cleared small sections of woodland for agriculture—about 0.8 hectares altogether (one had received agricultural grants for removing stumps); another is slowly reclaiming all his woods by removing trees from the edges as they die or become isolated through grazing. Two farmers have planted woods—one nineteen years ago and another five years ago, and four others are contemplating small-scale plantings for amenity under a county council-backed parish scheme. Woods are valued for shelter and occasional grazing. Eight farmers said they have not the time (or the money) to do anything with their woods: one is elderly and feels it beyond him, and one simply thought woods uneconomic relative to agricultural enterprises. Five expressed interest in grants for woodland management. In general, however, there is mostly apathy or indifference towards woods despite the fact that eleven of the seventeen farmers interviewed requested a second interview.

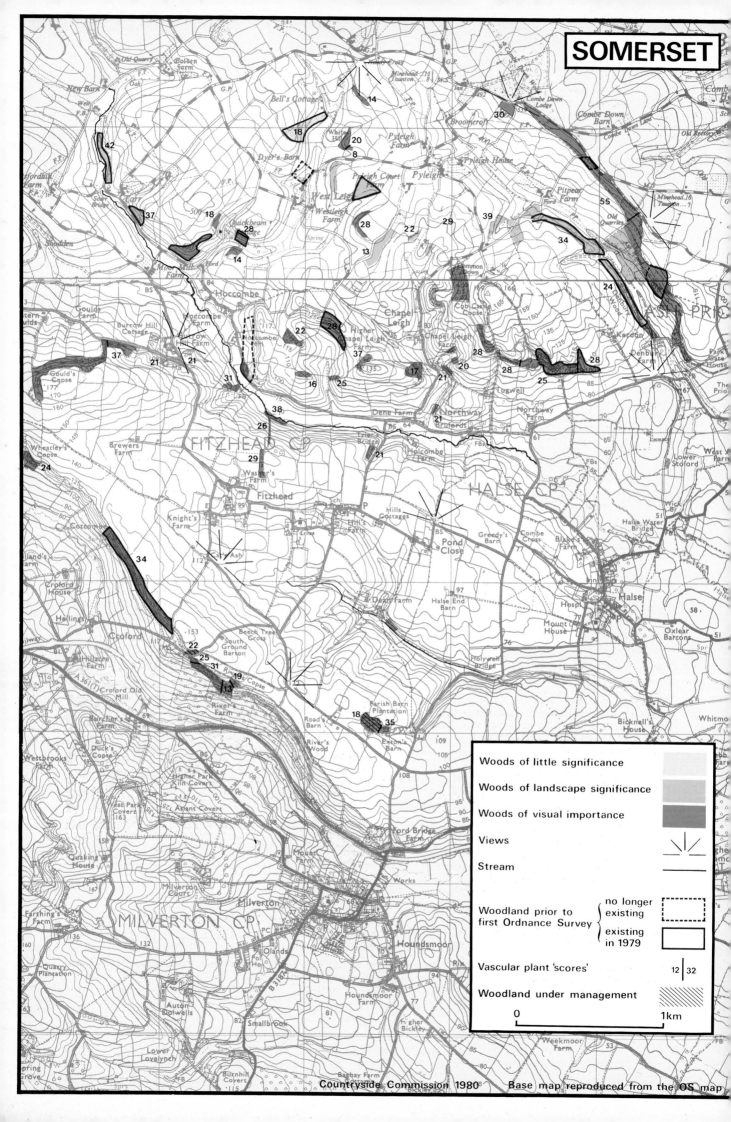

SOMERSET

Woods of little significance

Woods of landscape significance

Woods of visual importance

Views

Stream

Woodland prior to first Ordnance Survey { no longer existing / existing in 1979 }

Vascular plant 'scores' 12 | 32

Woodland under management

0   1km

Countryside Commission 1980   Base map reproduced from the OS map

Table H.2 Attitudes to Woods in the Somerset Study Area

	Woods/trees in general	Landscape	Wildlife	Game	Financial gain/loss
Strongly interested/ appreciative/anxious	4	4	—	—	—
Quite interested/ appreciative/anxious	11	7	9	3	2
Mildly interested appreciative/anxious	—	2	1	1	6
Indifferent	1	1	1	6	6
Antipathetic	—	2	3	6	2

The Woods

H.6   As the Map shows, the majority of the woods are on the smaller farms in the broken country to the north of the area. Woodlands to the south are all located on the steeper slopes. Separated by ownership and stand type, they break down into 49 units, two of which are managed and so were not surveyed. The generally small size of farms in the area is reflected in the woodland ownership: two farms have 5 woods each; two have 4; four have 3; seven have 2; and five have 1 wood. Table H.3 shows their size distribution.

Table H.3 Areas of Woods Surveyed in the Somerset Study Area

	Number of woods	Proportion of total (Base 47)
Less than 0.25 ha	8	17%
0.26 ha to 1 ha	28	60%
1.01 ha to 5 ha	10	21%
5.01 ha to 9.9 ha	1	2%
10 ha and over	—	—

H.7   The area of woodland has apparently increased since the old series Ordnance Survey maps by about 27 per cent. Virtually every wood surveyed contains at least one quarry and sometimes a whole series of them. They may have been associated with the many nearby lime kilns, the good condition of which suggests that they were in use until recent times. This in turn suggests that firing kilns was a traditional use for material from the older woods with newer ones springing up as the quarries were abandoned. Sweet chestnut is common in some woods, and was probably introduced for coppice.

H.8   The main local markets are for general-purpose saw-milling, with a large saw-mill within ten kilometres and five smaller ones within forty kilometres. Demand is high for oak and ash, and fair for other species. Road access is good, but cross-farm access difficult because of the topography and the small fields with their banks and hedges. There were no complaints about the number or the activities of contractors.

H.9   Tree and plant growth is very luxuriant in places but, as in the Cornwall study area, a slow deterioration due to grazing and holding stock in wet or cold weather is taking place. One wood used for holding pigs has totally lost its ground vegetation. Table H.4 shows something of the present character of the woods. One area shown on the current map as a wood scarcely has any tree cover. A number of older woods are shading out ground vegetation or alternatively are becoming 'park-like'. Much of the woodland is becoming derelict.

Useful timber, but poor understory reduces wildlife value

H.10   **Wildlife.** The vegetation appears to be characteristic of freely drained calcareous or flushed soils—dry ash-maple and ash-hazel woodlands. The Map shows the plant scores and their distribution: differences between woods are fairly high, reflecting their different ages and the present use or abuse. Badger setts were found in a number of woods and rabbits are numerous.

H.11   **Forestry and Timber.** The area is obviously capable of producing good timber but the general condition of woods is one of dereliction. Natural regeneration is largely absent, although there are exceptions which suggest that the cause may at least in part lie in the high population of rabbits. However, the maturity of much of the growth and the presence nearby of reasonable

93

Table H.4 Types of Woodland in the Somerset Study Area

		Number	Proportion
A.	Recently planted woodlands	2	4%
B.	Scrub woodland invasion	2	4%
C.	Secondary regrowth on areas clearfelled 30 to 40 years ago	1	2%
D.	Self-sown woods of mixed age trees and shrubs	2	4%
E.	Coppice wood with few and poor standards	9	18%
F.	Overgrown coppice with standards and 'stores'	18	37%
G.	Woods and parks of mature trees with no natural regeneration	10	20%
H.	Areas recently clearfelled but no new planting	1	2%
I.	Mature/semi-mature plantations (may have admixture of natural regeneration and coppice)	4	8%
J.	High forest of native spp (may have a few planted exotics)	—	—
K.	Coppice/coppice-with-standards in good condition	—	—

(Base 49)

markets is reflected in the valuations summarised in Table H.5. In round terms the total standing wood volume in the surveyed woods was estimated at 7,812 cubic metres, or 156 cubic metres per hectare, and the estimated average value, again in round terms, of this standing material was £1,117 per hectare, or £7.18 per cubic metre.

Table H.5 Quantities and Values of Forest Produce

Type of produce	Species	Quantity[1] (cu m)	Standing value (£)
Sawlogs	Oak	1,438	22,100
	Ash	1,057	17,553
	Beech	489	9,494
	Sweet Chestnut	207	2,209
	Elm	187	1,030
	Field Maple	17	95
	Sycamore	39	270
	Sitka Spruce	11	66
	Cherry	10	272
	Larch	6	55
	Other Conifer	4	25
	Sawlog totals	3,465	53,169
Firewood		5,843 tonnes[2]	2,922
	GRAND TOTAL		£56,091

[1]Rounded to nearest whole cubic metre
[2]Green weight

H.12 **Game.** Because of their location the game consultant felt that the woodlands would prove unlikely to be suitable for more than modest attempts at game management. Climatically the area is suitable for wild pheasant, but the relationship of the woodlands to the topography and to each other makes them difficult to 'drive'. In addition, with so much unmanaged woodland (and difficult terrain within it due to the numerous quarries), it would be difficult to control predators. To overcome the problems arising from the small size of holding, a considerable degree of co-operation between neighbouring farmers would be needed to make even rough shooting work well, and from the evidence of the interviews this would not be forthcoming.

Conclusion

H.13 The woods lie mostly on land which is difficult for agriculture—although there are plans to clear some areas for livestock grazing. However, the high frequency of grazing is already having its effects and over several more decades there are likely to be significant losses of trees and even whole woods. A high proportion of the woods are derelict or overmature, and in general a considerable amount of work and financial investment would be needed to improve their condition.

H.14 The impression is one of very varying attitudes to the woods. Some farmers are strongly sympathetic and others quite apathetic or even antagonistic. On the smaller holdings the farmers are too busy to think about managing their woods, and on the larger more prosperous holdings they have other things to do with their money. Nevertheless, there is a significant amount of goodwill and if practical help can be made available—perhaps by extending the Community Council's hedgerow and tree management scheme—then at least some of the decline may be arrested.

Warwickshire

Landscape

I.1   The Warwickshire study area was selected partly to have one in the West Midlands region, partly for its strong historical association with woods (it lies within what was once the Forest of Arden), and partly because it was thought desirable to have an area, (other than East Sussex) where there are signs of urban pressures. The western margin is only fourteen kilometres from the centre of Birmingham, and the eastern only eight kilometres from the centre of Coventry. The southern boundary is the M6 motorway, and the northern the Birmingham to Leicester railway. Other boundaries are minor roads and a stream.

I.2   Despite these influences, it is a pleasant piece of countryside with many winding lanes, neatly kept hedges, fairly small fields of red soil, and attractive sandstone buildings. The road system is complex, and despite the absence of villages within the area its population is fairly high. The whole area shelves gently from the Atherstone-Corley Ridge towards the River Teme to the west and is dissected by streams, making an undulating landscape. There are fairly extensive views into the area from the motorway, and numerous more local viewpoints along the internal roads. The area is popular with many (mainly local) people for weekend and holiday recreation, especially day visits by car.

I.3   The area covers about 1,900 hectares, of which 66.7 hectares are woodland all of which, apart from 0.2 hectares, are unmanaged. Virtually all the remainder is farmland. It was not possible to get complete information on the number of farms, but we were in contact with twenty-three farmers or landowners with holdings in the area. The pattern of farm size and ownership is shown in Table I.1. The farms are predominantly small and owner-occupied.

Table I.1   Size and Ownership of Farms in the Warwickshire Study Area

	20 ha & below	21–40 ha	41–60 ha	61–80 ha	81–100 ha	Over 100 ha
Number of farms	6	6	2	2	—	4
Proportion of total (Base 20)	30%	30%	10%	10%	—	20%

(Owner-occupiers[1]   16)
(Tenants[1]   4)
(No information   2)
(Refusals   3)
(No Contact   1)

[1]Farmers may both own and rent land in the area

I.4   The geology of the area is one of Carboniferous Red Marls and Sandstone with a small deposit of Boulder Clay to the south-west, giving rise to light, fertile and very productive soils up to Class 2 standard. The farming is very mixed in character, with arable (cereals, potatoes, market vegetables), dairying, beef, sheep, pigs and poultry. Other land-based enterprises include a kennels and cattery, Christmas tree growing and a nudist club.

The Farmers

I.5   Of the twenty-three farmers and estate owners in the area with whom we were in contact, eight had no woods. Three refused a first interview (or were uninformative). Only three requested a second interview. None of the farmers interviewed is contemplating any management of their woods. One of them plans to clear his woods for agriculture. Very little woodland produce is taken but a number of woods are used for game rearing or shelter. The attitudes of the farmers (Table I.2) are mixed but with a strong level of indifference toward most aspects of woodlands. The overall impression is of a highly aware but preoccupied group of people.

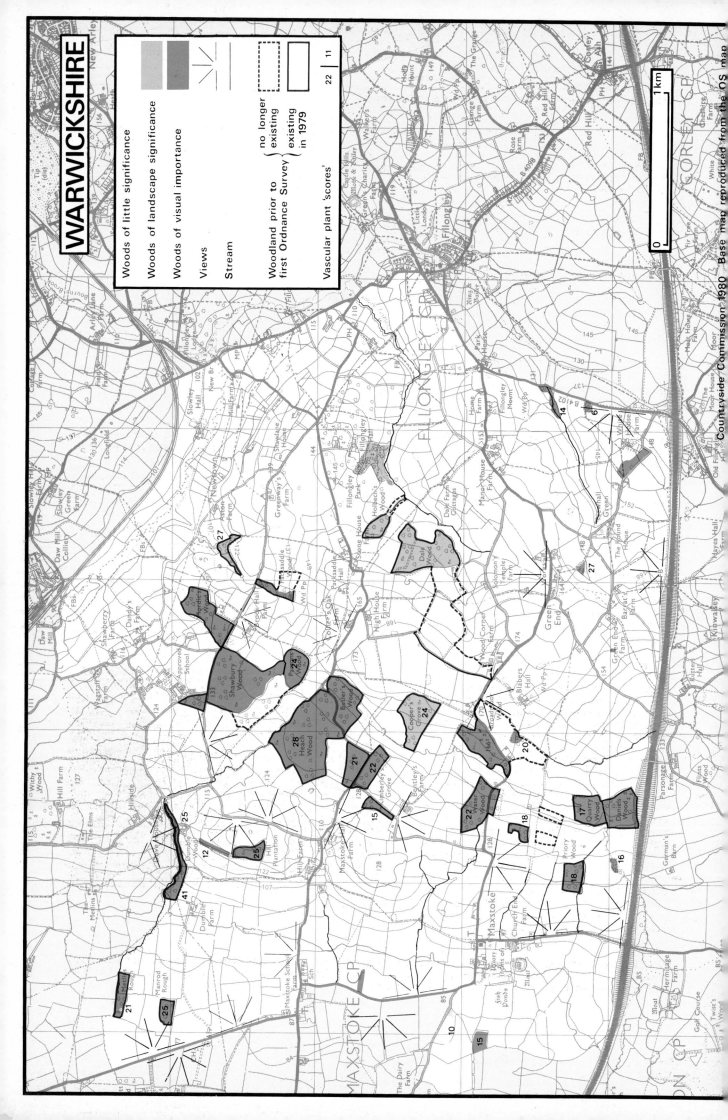

WARWICKSHIRE

Woods of little significance

Woods of landscape significance

Woods of visual importance

Views

Stream

Woodland prior to first Ordnance Survey { no longer existing / existing in 1979 }

Vascular plant 'scores'

22 | 11

0 ___ 1 km

Countryside Commission 1980 Base map reproduced from the OS map

Table I.2 Attitudes to Woods in the Warwickshire Study Area

	Woods/trees in general	Landscape	Wildlife	Game	Financial gain/loss
Strongly interested/ appreciative/anxious	7	2	1	—	—
Quite interested/ appreciative/anxious	6	9	8	5	8
Mildly interested/ appreciative/anxious	2	4	6	8	6
Indifferent	6	6	6	7	7
Antipathetic	1	1	1	2	1

The Woods

I.6   The location of the woods can be clearly seen from the Map. Most are substantial blocks of land, lying north-south down the middle of the area, with small outliers. Divided by ownership and stand type, they number 31. One estate has 12 woods 'in hand'; two farmers have 4 woods each; two have 2 woods; and seven have 1 wood each.

Table I.3   Areas of Woods Surveyed in the Warwickshire Study Area

	Number of woods	Proportion of total (Base 30)
Less than 0.25 ha	4	13%
0.26 ha to 1 ha	9	30%
1.01 ha to 5 ha	14	47%
5.01 ha to 9.9 ha	2	7%
10 ha and over	1	3%

I.7   Changes in woodland cover since the last century appear to be considerable, with a 57 per cent reduction in area, mostly cleared for agriculture. However, there does not appear to have been any reclamation within the lifespan or tenure of the respondents. From the old maps and from the physical evidence (such as the undulating edges to the larger woods) they may be of some antiquity. Traditional uses for timber must have been varied, but most woods appear at one time or another to have been under coppice-type management: they would have probably provided produce for both local craft and industrial uses. At present there are markets for all types of timber, and there is a good deal of competition for quality sawlogs, with seventeen firms listed in Warwickshire, Leicestershire and Staffordshire[35]. There are also markets for turnery poles and there is evidence of a demand for firewood. With the nearby motorway system, the many minor roads in the area, and the light soils, access is good to most of the woods surveyed. The respondents were unable to supply any information on contractors.

Fine oak standards in neglected coppice

I.8   The area appears well suited to the production of good timber, having some of the finest oak and ash seen during the study. It has felt the impact of Dutch elm disease but does not show too much sign of it, except in one patch to the south-east. The general types of woodland in the area are detailed in Table I.4.

Table I.4   Types of Woodland in the Warwickshire Study Area

		Number	*Proportion*
A.	Recently planted woodlands	1	3%
B.	Scrub woodland invasion	—	—
C.	Secondary regrowth on areas clearfelled 30 to 40 years ago	2	6%
D.	Self-sown woods of mixed age trees and shrubs	3	10%
E.	Coppice wood with few and poor standards	2	6%
F.	Overgrown coppice with standards and 'stores'	6	19%
G.	Woods and parks of mature trees with no natural regeneration	2	6%
H.	Areas recently clearfelled but no new planting	—	—
I.	Mature/semi-mature plantations (may have admixture of natural regeneration and coppice)	5	16%
J.	High forest of native spp. (may have a few planted exotics)	7	23%
K.	Coppice/coppice-with-standards in good condition	3	10%
			(Base 31)

I.9   **Wildlife.** The woodland species appear to be intermediate between ash-hazel and ash-maple stand groups, with a strong component of alder, which suggests some impeded drainage at lower root level (perhaps falling into the acid pedunculate oak-ash-hazel stand type). It is hard to read much of a pattern into the plant scores (see Map) but they accord well with the apparent age and sizes of the woods. One of the woodlands is a Site of Special Scientific Interest—mainly because of its mosses. The presence of badgers and of fallow deer was noted.

I.10   **Forestry and Timber.** Except for East Sussex, the woods in this area are in better physical condition than in any other area studied. In part this is a result of the heavy felling of mature timber which took place during World War II. Since then the regrowth of the coppice into good sized stems has produced woods with good age and species distributions, and the older stems have had ample light (and protection from grazing) to grow into what are now quite valuable woods. Although more than one owner asserted that "there is nothing left in there—all the good timber was removed during the war", in fact, the total standing wood volume in these unmanaged woods was estimated, in round terms, at 7,149 cubic metres—an average of 108 cubic metres per hectare—and the average estimated values were £1,969 per hectare or £18.31 per cubic metre. Table I.5 gives further details.

Table I.5   Quantities and Values of Forest Produce

Type of produce	*Species*	*Quantity[1] (cu m)*	*Standing value (£)*
Sawlogs	Oak	2,407	106,444
	Ash	239	9,881
	Sycamore	21	175
	Elm	28	1,033
	Sweet Chestnut	91	4,192
	Alder	175	1,455
	Poplar	159	1,321
	Cherry	10	1,360
	Rowan	57	475
	Scots Pine	23	349
	Sawlog totals	3,210	126,685
Turnery Poles		1,257 tonnes[2]	2,514
Firewood		3,457 tonnes[2]	1,729
		GRAND TOTAL	**£130,928**

[1]Rounded to nearest whole cubic metre
[2]Green weight

I.11   However, the woods are beginning to get a neglected look about them. One owner had apparently rejected the advice of the Forestry Commission to replant with Douglas fir (for reasons unstated) but has done nothing since then. Two owners complained of poor work done by timber contractors. The three owners who asked for a second interview wanted to be advised on their options for future management and finance.

I.12 **Game.** There is little or no recent history of any committed game conservation in the area: there are no professional gamekeepers, for example, and what activity there is is small-scale. Most farmers or owners shoot over their woods but this tends to be only "for the pot". The extent of the woodland cover, the climate, topography, soils and agricultural mix, all make the area very suitable for game-rearing or re-stocking. Pheasants, partridge, woodcock, hare and rabbit are all present (as are fallow deer, noted previously). However, the small size of most holdings, the lack of more than a passing interest in improvement, and the proximity of the large cities (with the problem of poachers), make pheasant rearing a doubtful proposition. Provided that public access can be kept low, there is some potential for managing the wild fallow deer of the area as game.

Conclusion

I.13 Relative to the other areas in the study the woods are reasonably healthy and well-stocked, although most of them have reached the stage where more light and air is needed if their relatively good condition is to be maintained. Indeed, with wise management their value could be improved all round. They are also reasonably stable in the landscape. However, unlike most of the study areas, they are on land which appears quite usable for agriculture, and so the situation could change. Despite their nearness to Birmingham and Coventry there is little evidence that recreation is causing any problems, the many visitors to the area apparently being content to admire this very pleasant small-scale landscape from their cars.

Appendix III

Glossary

Broadleaved	Correctly, this applies to tree species which do not have needle-like leaves. Used in this report in its vernacular sense, it applies to tree species which are not coniferous, (ie are not members of the order of Coniferae or, indeed, of the gymnospermous plants generally).
Butt sweep	Pronounced curvature in one direction where the tree stem rises from the ground.
Cambium	A layer of growth cells which form bast to the outside and wood on the inside.
Canopy	The uppermost layer of woodland structure. Usually from 8m–30m above ground. Contains the standard, emergent and understorey trees.
Clearout, clearfell	Complete cutting of all trees to ground level over a significant area. (As distinct from group felling, selective felling or thinning.)
Coniferous	Tree species of the order Coniferae. Usually evergreen with needle-foliage.
Conversion	The cutting of a felled tree into useable products.
Coppice	Broadleaved wood which is cut over at regular intervals to produce a number of shoots from each stool. Also known as copse. To cut the shoots from a stool so that more will regrow.
Coppice with standards	The growing of trees to timber size at wide spacing amongst other trees and shrubs managed as coppice.
Cord	A volume of stacked logs, usually 2.4m × 1.2m × 1.2m, but varying in different districts. To cut wood to cord lengths and to stack it in cords.
Coupe	A coppice plot cut on a regular basis or a clear-felled area in a plantation. Also known as a panel.
Crown	The spreading branches and foliage of a tree.
Crown thinning	The careful removal of trees whose crowns are inhibiting the growth of other trees selected to be the final crop.
Edge effect	The special circumstances of light and microclimate where trees end and open ground begins.
Epicormic shoots	Shoots forming from dormant buds on the stem of a tree (usually when the light reaching the trunk is increased). They are usually regarded as reducing the value of timber due to knot formation.
Felled measure	The measurement of the stem timber lengths of a tree after felling and initial conversion. By extension, the term as applied to the practice of mutually agreeing to delay the final pricing of a tree crop until felling is completed and the value can be more accurately assessed.
Flushed soils	Soils with a considerable movement of water through the soil.
Form	The straightness and degree of taper of a tree stem.
Group felling/group system	A management system based on the successive opening and replanting of clearings within a wood. It reduces the impact of harvesting operations on the landscape and wildlife and retains the special microclimate of the wood.
High forest	Woodland dominated by full-grown trees suitable for timber.
Hoppus foot	Obsolescent unit of measurement for the cubic contents of round timber equal to 0.086 cubic metre.
Maiden stems	Trees which have grown from seed or root-suckers (as distinct from 'stores').
Management	The manipulation of a wood, through felling, planting and other operations to achieve desired objectives.
Microclimate	The conditions of temperature, atmosphere, moisture etc prevailing within a few feet of the ground (and thus experienced by a seedling tree for instance).

Monoculture	The practice of growing one crop species only (such as wheat or spruce) over a substantial area.
Overwood	Vernacular expression for branchwood or for the canopy.
Planking	Used here as an expression of the likely quality of timber in a tree (as distinct from and superior to 'fencing' or 'mining timber' quality).
Plant score	The total count of native vascular plant species in any wood, used *in any one study area* as a measure of the relative richness of the flora.
Pollard	A tree which is cut at 2m–4m above ground level then allowed to grow again to produce a crop of branches. To cut the branches from such a tree so that they will regrow.
Relict woodland	Woodland which has survived (even in a modified form) from the original forest cover pre-dating human settlement and clearance.
Rigg and furrow	A method of medieval ploughing which left the field surface in waves. In a woodland it is evidence that the wood is not 'relict'.
Scrub	In ecology, an area dominated by shrubs, possibly as a stage in succession to high forest. In forestry, an area of unproductive woodland.
Selection system	A management system which removes only single trees from every part of a wood each time a harvesting operation is carried out. The impact on landscape and wildlife is thus minimised but it requires a high order of skill to operate properly.
Seral	Pertaining to the succession of plant communities which occupy a site over a long period of time. (Implies that the current vegetation is not in equilibrium with the physical conditions prevailing on a site.)
Shelterwood system	A management system which after harvesting the main crop leaves a thin canopy which lets through enough light to reach the woodland flora to regenerate (through planting or natural seeding) the next tree crop. Leaves a wood little changed visually but tends to favour those species which can stand shade conditions over those which cannot. Can be 'regular' or 'irregular' depending on how evenly the sites of tree removal are located over the wood as a whole.
Smallwood	Forest produce which is not specifically timber. By extension, a standing crop which is not big enough to be used for timber.
Standard	A tree suitable for timber. A transplanted tree with 1.8m or more clear stem. In woodland structure a tree forming the dominant layer of the canopy. (See also 'coppice—with standards').
Stocking density	Number of trees per unit of area.
Stool shoots	Coppice shoots. Shoots sent up after cutting a tree to near ground level from dormant buds at the side of the stool or stump, or from adventitious buds from the cambium at the cut surface.
Stores	Coppice shoots singled out to grow on to timber size (ie all but one stem are cut away from the stool).
Suppression	Trees and shrubs moribund in growth due to shade or root competition.
Sustained yield	A steady supply of forest produce from a managed forest, whereby the total removed never exceeds (except in the very short term) the annual growth between harvesting operations. (Analogous to spending the interest but leaving the capital intact.)
Tail corn	Traditionally the grain which fell out of the end or 'tail' of a threshing machine. Low quality grain which has only a limited sale value.
Understorey	Trees and shrubs whose crowns are below those of the dominant trees.
Underwood	Understorey trees and shrubs looked at as potential forest produce.
Vascular plants	Plants having roots and stems which are composed of bundles of conducting vessels. (As distinct from fungi and lichens for example.)
Wildwood	Relict woods. Woods which have survived in their present location from the prehistoric woodland cover. (As distinct from woods, of whatever age, which originally were plantations.)
Yield Class	The maximum rate of growth of timber volume per year which can be obtained at a site. Usually obtained from Forestry Commission 'General Yield Tables' (based on tree heights and ages). Broadly speaking it is the estimated sustained yield which could be obtained under intensive management.

Appendix IV

References

1 Advisory Council for Agriculture and Horticulture in England and Wales *Agriculture and the Countryside.* Ministry of Agriculture, Fisheries and Food. 1978.

2 Agricultural Development and Advisory Service *Wildlife Conservation in Semi-natural Habitats on Farms.* Ministry of Agriculture, Fisheries and Food. HMSO. 1975.

3 Appleton, J *The Experience of Landscape.* Wiley. 1975.

4 Brasnett, N U *Planned Management of Forests.* George Allen and Unwin. 1953.

5 Carson, R *Silent Spring.* Crest Books. 1962.

6 Centre for Agricultural Strategy *A Forestry Strategy for the UK.* Discussion paper for conference held at University of Reading on 26 April 1979.

7 Countryside Commission *New Agricultural Landscapes: Issues, Objectives and Action.* Countryside Commission. CCP 102. 1977.

8 Countryside Review Committee *The Countryside: Problems and Policies.* HMSO. 1976.

9 Dartington Amenity Research Trust *Local Authority Amenity Tree Planting Schemes: A Report to the Countryside Commission.* July 1976.

10 Davidson, J and R Lloyd (eds) *Conservation and Agriculture.* John Wiley & Sons Ltd. 1977.

11 Denby, A W 'The Location of Forest-based Industries'. Proceedings of conference: *The Future of Upland Britain,* held at Reading, September 1977. Centre for Agricultural Strategy. 1978.

12 Department of Education and Science *Forestry, Agriculture and Marginal Land.* Report by the Natural Resources (Technical) Committee. HMSO. 1957.

13 Department of Education and Science *Forestry, Agriculture and the Multiple Use of Rural Land.* Report by the Land Use Study Group. HMSO. 1966.

14 Department of the Environment *Sinews for Survival.* A report to the UN Conference on the Human Environment, Stockholm, June 1972. HMSO. 1972.

15 Development Commission *Thirty-fourth Report of the Development Commissioners.* HMSO. December 1976.

16 Dickinson, G C *Maps and Air Photographs.* Edward Arnold. 1969.

17 Edlin, H L *Forestry and Woodland Life.* Batsford. 1947.

18 Edlin, H L *Woodland Crafts in Britain.* Batsford. 1949.

19 Edlin, H L *Forestry in Great Britain: A Review of Progress to 1972.* Forestry Commission. 1972.

20 Eyre, S R *Vegetation and Soils.* E Arnold. 1968.

21 Forestry Commission *Advice for Woodland Owners.* Forestry Commission. 1977.

22 Forestry Commission *Census of Woodlands, 1965–67.* Forestry Commission. 1970.

23 Forestry Commission *Forestry in the Weald.* Forestry Commission. Booklet No. 22. 1968.

24 Forestry Commission *Forest Management Tables (Metric).* Forestry Commission. Booklet No. 34. 1971.

25 Forestry Commission *Forest Mensuration Handbook.* Forestry Commission. Booklet No. 39. 1975.

26 Forestry Commission *Poplar Cultivation.* Forestry Commission. Leaflet No. 27. 1963.

27 Forestry Commission *The Wood Production Outlook in Britain: A Review.* Forestry Commission. 1978.

28 Gane, M *Priorities in Planning.* Commonwealth Forestry Institute. Paper No. 43. University of Oxford. 1969.

29	Gibson, E J	*Principles of Perceptual Learning and Development.* Appleton Century. 1969.
30	Gray, N	(a) 'Pheasants and Forestry'. Paper given to Monks Wood Symposium No. 6 on *Lowland Forestry and Wildlife Conservation,* held by the Nature Conservancy, 4/5 May 1972. (b) 'Specialist Recreation—Shooting'. Paper to conference on *Recreation and the Woodland Owner* at Beaconsfield, 16 October 1972.
31	Hart, C E	(a) *Timber Prices and Forestry Costings.* Published by the author. 1975. (b) *British Timber Prices and Forestry Costings.* Published by the author. 1979.
32	Hart, C E	*Taxation of Woodlands.* Published by the author. 1979.
33	HM Treasury	*Forestry in Great Britain.* An inter-departmental cost-benefit study. HMSO. 1972.
34	HM Treasury	*Rural Depopulation.* Report by an inter-departmental group. HMSO. 1976.
35	Home Grown Timber Merchants Association	*Annual Report, 1977.*
36	Hunter, J	'Conserving the Countryside Legacy', in *Country Life.* 30 June 1977.
37	Jobling, J and M L Pearce	*Free Growth of Oak.* Forestry Commission. Forest Record 113. HMSO. 1977.
38	Johnston, D R, A J Grayson and R T Bradley	*Forest Planning.* Faber and Faber. 1967.
39	Jones, G R	Personal communication.
40	Lennard, W (transl) and M Gane (ed)	*Martin Faustmann and the Evolution of Discounted Cash Flow.* Commonwealth Forestry Institute. Paper No. 42. 1968.
41	Leonard, P L and R O Cobham	'The Farming Landscape of England and Wales: a Changing Scene', in *Landscape Planning.* Elsevier Scientific Publ Co. Amsterdam. 1977.
42	Linton, D L	'The Assessment of Scenery as a Natural Resource', in *'Scottish Geographical Magazine* Vol 84, No. 3. December 1968.
43	Lloyd, R J and G P Wibberley	'Agricultural Change', in *Conservation and Agriculture,* Ed J Davidson and R Lloyd. John Wiley & Sons Ltd. 1977.
44	Lowenthal, D and H C Prince	'English Landscape Tastes', in *Geographical Review* Vol LV, No. 2. American Geographical Society. 1965.
45	MacEwen, M	'A New Farming Landscape?', in *Country Life,* 25 December 1975.
46	Mather, A S	'Patterns of Afforestation in Britain since 1945', in *Geography* Vol 63, Part 3. July 1978.
47	Ministry of Agriculture, Fisheries and Food	*A Century of Agricultural Statistics 1866–1966.* Ministry of Agriculture, Fisheries and Food and Department of Agriculture and Fisheries for Scotland. HMSO. 1968.
48	Ministry of Agriculture, Fisheries and Food	*UK Food and Farming in Figures.* Ministry of Agriculture, Fisheries and Food and Government Statistical Service. 1978.
49	Mitchell, A F	'Forests in the Landscape', in *Silviculture and Good Landscapes in British Forestry.* M H Orrom and A F Mitchell. Forestry Commission Research and Development Paper No. 91. July 1972.
50	Moore, N	'Conservation and Agriculture', in *Naturopa.* 1977.
51	Moore, N W and M D Hooper	'On the Number of Bird Species in British Woods', in *Biological Conservation* Vol B. 1975.
52	Moore, N W	'The Scientific, Wildlife and Education Benefits of Woods of Varying Ages and Sizes'. Proceedings of conference on *The Future of the Small Woodland,* Peak National Park Study Centre. 29 March 1976.
53	Neisser, V	*Cognitive Psychology.* Appleton Century. 1967.
54	Newby, H, C Bell, P Saunders and D Rose	*The Attitudes of East Anglian Farmers.* Report on survey conducted by the Department of Sociology, University of Essex. 1977.
55	Osmaston, F C	*The Management of Forests.* George Allen and Unwin. 1968.
56	Page, G	'Some Effects of Conifer Crops on Soil Properties', in *Commonwealth Forestry Review* Vol 47 (1), No. 131. March 1968.

57	Page, R	*The Decline of an English Village*. Davis-Poynter. 1975.
58	Peterken, G F	'A Method of Assessing Woodland Flora for Conservation Using Indicator Species', in *Biological Conservation* Vol 6, No. 4. October 1974.
59	Peterken, G F and P T Harding	'Woodland Conservation in Eastern England: Comparing the Effects of Changes in Three Study Areas since 1946', in *Biological Conservation* Vol 8. 1975.
60	Peterken, G F	'Habitat Conservation Priorities in British and European Woodlands', in *Biological Conservation* Vol 11. 1977.
61	Peterken, G F	'General Management Principles for Nature Conservation in British Woodlands', in *Forestry* Vol L, No. 1. 1977.
62	Peterken, G F	*Stand Types in British Semi-natural Woodland*. FST Notes 11 (Provisional Appendix). Nature Conservancy Council. April 1978.
63	Rackham, O	*Trees and Woodlands in the British Landscape*. J M Dent & Sons Ltd. 1976.
64	Rose, W	*The Village Carpenter*. Cambridge University Press. 1937.
65	Severin, T	*The Brendan Voyage*. Hutchinson & Co. 1978.
66	Simpson, L M	'The Extent and Composition of Existing Broadleaved Woodland in Britain', in supplement on 'Management of Broadleaved Woodlands', *Forestry*. April 1974.
67	Sturt, G	*The Wheelwright's Shop*. Cambridge University Press. 1923.
68	Timber Development Association	*World Timbers* Vol 1. Timber Development Association. 1962.
69	Treasure, B	'Hardwood is Forgotten in Commercial Building', in *Building Trades Journal*. 22 June 1979.
70	Troup, R S	*Silvicultural Systems* 2nd Edition. Ed E W Jones. Clarendon Press. 1952.
71	Tubbs, C R	'Woodlands: Their History and Conservation', in *Conservation in Practice*. Warren, A and F B Goldsmith (eds).
72	Vesey-Fitzgerald, B	*It's My Delight*. Eyre and Spottiswoode. 1947.
73	Warren, A and F B Goldsmith (ed)	*Conservation in Practice*. John Wiley & Sons. 1974.
74	Westmacott, R and T Worthington	*New Agricultural Landscapes*. Countryside Commission. CCP 76. 1974.
75	Worthington, T R	*The Landscapes of Institutional Landowners*. Countryside Commission. Working Paper No. 18. 1979.

Printed in England for Her Majesty's Stationery Office by Linneys of Mansfield
Dd. 8220105 3M 12/82